THE

Entrepreneurial
CONSPIRACY

*Six Behaviors That Conspire to
Derail Your Company*

CHUCK VIOLAND

© Chuck Violand 2021

Print ISBN: 978-1-54398-489-7
eBook ISBN: 978-1-54398-490-3

To my loving wife, Karen

CONTENTS

ACKNOWLEDGEMENTS

While there are so many people who contributed to or had an impact on this book, there is one group that stands out among them and without whom this book could not have been written. It is with profound gratitude that I recognize the hundreds of clients who trusted me enough to invite me into their businesses and their lives. Without their trust and openness, I would never had been able to identify the behaviors that serve as the basis for this book.

I would also like to recognize the significant and invaluable contribution of my collaborator in writing this book, Tim Kraft, who fleshed out much of the raw material I presented and brought it to life with his skillful pen. His ability to help me think through the concepts and to massage them into a coherent narrative is something beyond my own abilities.

Just as with the clients who shared their stories with me, this book could not have been written without the thousands of people at countless conventions and tradeshows who sat and listened as I presented the material that served as the basis for this book. Their interactions as I presented, and their comments following, allowed me to explore each of the concepts more deeply.

My colleagues at Violand Management Associates have had a far greater impact on this book than they may realize. Not only have they been patient with me as I've talked about "the book," but they helped to refine the concepts by challenging me to explain and defend them.

Of course, no acknowledgement would be complete without recognizing the unwavering support of my wife, Karen. She is the love of my life and the one who patiently listened as I waxed on for years about these behaviors, knowing that what I was really doing was thinking them through with my mouth open, after which she would offer her keen insights and priceless suggestions. But, without a doubt, her most valuable contribution was her saintly patience as I talked about the impact these behaviors had on other people and her restraint as she recognized them in me. For her I am eternally grateful.

FOREWORD

S ome people might refer to me as a serial entrepreneur, having started and operated a number of small businesses, including a cleaning and restoration company. While none of my businesses became the kind you read about in popular business magazines, each one provided me with invaluable, and often costly, lessons in what NOT to do. In 1987, I made the transition from performing cleaning and restoration services to helping others improve and grow their businesses. In doing so, I had the good fortune to stumble into a career where I occupied a very privileged seat behind the scenes with these hardworking entrepreneurs.

As I began my new role, I wrote articles in trade publications and made presentations at meetings and conferences, sharing what I'd learned from my business experiences. Some of what I had to say obviously hit home with people who read my articles or heard me speak, because I started getting calls. Business owners would invite me to take a look around their company and search for areas where they might be able to make improvements. Some of these companies were already doing well when I was asked in; others were in pretty poor shape; and a few were teetering on the brink of insolvency.

At times, the process of exploring their business situation was painful for these owners. They had to open their books and bare their soul to give me a clear picture of what they were doing well and what improvements could be made. Few people enjoy having strangers root around their metaphorical closets or rifle through the underwear drawers of their organization. Regardless of what I found or the level of success we achieved, I applaud these owners for having the courage to invite me in. I got to look in the dark places most business owners don't share with outsiders. Based on what I found, I offered them my best advice about what changes to make to improve things in their business.

It didn't take long before I began to notice patterns emerge. These patterns repeated from business to business, profoundly affecting their success. Surprisingly, these patterns had little to do with market dynamics or economic trends and almost everything to do with the behaviors of the owner. Based on our investigation, we would agree to a specific set of business initiatives that might include implementing marketing and sales strategies, streamlining inefficient operating processes, or installing financial controls to improve profitability and cash flow. These initiatives were almost always successful, but the success frequently didn't last. More often than not, things soon would start to unravel and return to their previous state.

What went wrong? The initiatives were sound, proven, and tailored to the business. Why couldn't their initial success be sustained? What forces were conspiring against the increased success of these businesses?

We drilled down into the reversals and tried to identify their root causes. As we did so, it became apparent that the source of many of the companies' issues weren't systems- or strategy-oriented. The problem wasn't new competition or market shifts. In most cases, the early successes were undone by the behaviors of the company's owners or senior managers. Our thoughtfully considered and carefully implemented improvements were undone by the very people most interested and involved in implementing the changes; those who had the greatest stake in the business's continued success.

I realized then that some of the very traits and behaviors that drove these people to launch their business, behaviors that may have been strengths in the early stages and enabled them to achieve initial growth, became weaknesses in the long run and were sabotaging their long-term success.

When I present The Entrepreneurial Conspiracy to live audiences, the response during the presentation is almost always alarming to me. Most attendees watch me with a blank expression on their face, which is unnerving for any presenter. I assume I'm not connecting with them, that I've missed the mark and they don't see how the material is relevant. But after I'm done and they come up to talk to me, I realize the reason they are stone-faced and silent is that the concepts actually do hit home with many and catch many of them by surprise. The problem isn't that there is nothing in the presentation that they can relate to, but rather that they are struck by how much of it does relate to them.

Getting to Know You

The consulting model I've always used when working with my clients is a very hands-on, personal one. I don't show up with a standard punch list of items that should be addressed, although after more than 30 years of working with clients I could probably put together a pretty good list. Instead, I have come to learn that every business, every market, and most importantly, every owner, is different. To uncover the unique problems and potential of each client, we spend time talking about the aspirations they have for their beloved business, the operational issues they face, and the business challenges they confront. Only then can we create a customized strategy to grow ... or to save ... their business.

In working so closely with these owners, we got to know each other on a personal level. We shared stories about our kids, talked about great adventures we'd had and look forward to having, and expressed our views on life and the world. Regarding business, we came to understand one another's motivations and concerns about being a small business owner. We learned about the things that excite and frighten us and what drives us to want our business to succeed.

In working with all these wonderful clients, I was able to uncover the recurring behaviors that could, and sometimes would, be their undoing. I identified six specific, named behaviors that could be compared to The Force in the *Star Wars* movies. These behaviors were positive, powerful, and could be tremendously valuable to building business success. But these same behaviors also have a dark side. If not harnessed and channeled to positive use, they invariably wreak havoc on a business.

Despite my best efforts to provide clients with guidance and systems to address their current problems or enhance a successful business, these six behaviors interacted and conspired to drag some companies down. At best, the business never lived up to the owner's expectations or delivered on their dreams; at worst, the business failed and left the owner with nothing but debt and regret.

When naming this book, I chose the word *conspiracy* carefully. A conspiracy is, by definition, hidden from view. Those being conspired against are unaware that forces are secretly colluding to bring about their undoing. Most entrepreneurs are unaware that the six behaviors we'll explore are, even now, working to slow the growth of their business, alienate employees, and ultimately bring about financial ruin.

But all is not lost. There's still hope.

The ancient Chinese general, Sun Tzu, said, "If you know the enemy and know yourself, you need not fear the result of a hundred battles." When it comes to the problem of entrepreneurial behavior, I might also quote another, more recent expert, Pogo. "We have met the enemy and he is us."

You can be your own worst enemy when it comes to growing your business. Fortunately, you don't need to be. In this book, I will give examples to help you identify the behaviors that conspire to destroy you and other entrepreneurs, and I will offer practical solutions to overcome the Entrepreneurial Conspiracy.

Overview

According to the Small Business Administration, about 98% of all businesses in America, or about 23 million of them, are small businesses that generate less than $20 million in annual revenue. These are remarkable numbers, and they include my own company.

In some cases, we start a company simply because we make a lousy employee. We get fed up taking direction from someone we feel isn't as qualified as we are to run the business. We get frustrated by the fact that no one recognizes our brilliant ideas for improvements. This frustration can gnaw at our insides and often erupts in ways that aren't conducive to continued employment. The best way to maintain an income in this case is to create our own job, eliminating the possibility of being written up or fired by our boss. In fact, according to research conducted by the U.S. Census Bureau, almost 78% of all businesses registered in the U.S. have no employees other than the owner. That's a lot of solo operators!

Sometimes people strike out and start a business because they are bored. They want to do something different and rather than try to find a job that meets their requirements, they create their own job.

Most small businesses, though, start because the entrepreneur has a particular passion, an aspiration or vision for a product, a pastime, or a skill. They may work for a company that is aligned with that passion, but as an employee they become frustrated when their manager fails to do things to the level of quality that customers deserve. These employees decide "I can do this better" and set off on their own.

The businesses started by these individuals are, in many ways and on many levels, lifestyle businesses. Their founders typically grow them to their own levels of confidence, competence, and comfort. As such, they are direct reflections of their founders. The founder's influence may also be mirrored in the fundamental traits of the business, such as the desired size of the company they choose to create. Most entrepreneurs don't launch their business with the intention of becoming the next Microsoft, Zappos, or Dell, although some may think they have the next big idea that just might turn into something huge. Still, they launch the enterprise with some idea about its eventual, optimal scale.

For some, entrepreneurship is literally a matter of faith. They create a business that provides them with the freedom to live their values, promote their faith, or allow them time for volunteer or missionary work.

Regardless of what drove them to choose the entrepreneurial path, you can see their values take shape in the behaviors related to how they operate their business. How do they interact with their customers, employees, and suppliers? Do they treat them with respect or disdain? What types of customers do they try to attract to their business? Are they interested in building lifelong relationships or simply making a big sale and moving on?

What kind of employees do they seek out and hire? Do they focus on hiring the right technical skills, or is personality a more valued trait? If an owner is disciplined and focused, they will tend to attract workers who are similarly disciplined and focused. Not every one of them will be and certainly not to the same degree as the owner; but by and large they will share the same traits as the owner. Either that or they won't be around for long.

Aside from hiring, the owner's values shape many other behaviors pertaining to critical business functions. Regarding finance, for example, will the business adhere to the strictest standards of financial practices, or is the owner comfortable operating in grey areas if it will mean a significant boost to the bottom line? The behavior of the business reflects the behavior of the owner; the two are inseparable.

The owner's values also exhibit themselves in the most mundane behaviors, such as how tidy they keep their office or work area and their expectations for how employees will maintain their own workspaces.

So, if a business is a reflection of the owner, and the owner is a reflection of their values, then it's clear that the business will be dramatically affected by the behaviors of the owner, whether good or bad.

Humans have an unlimited number of behavioral characteristics that shape our identity. When we happen to own a business, these behaviors help to shape the characteristics of the business as well—especially when it's a small business where the personal behaviors of everyone in the company have a heightened impact on its performance. Of that unlimited number, there are a handful I've observed with entrepreneurs that seem to reappear on a regular basis. Those behaviors are the focus of this book.

The entrepreneurial behaviors are:

- Blurred Vision
- No Accountability
- Heroic Managing
- E-Drift
- Hiding Out
- Swollen Ego

While all these behaviors sound like negatives, most of them are positives, at least in the early years of a business. As our company grows, these behaviors are reinforced and strengthened because they were, to a significant degree, responsible for our early success.

But behaviors that were beneficial to a small business can stymie a growing one. Strengths turn into weaknesses, and those weaknesses matter greatly to the continued growth of the business.

Anyone who's grown herbs in the garden or a pot on the windowsill knows that when the plant is young, it benefits from being pinched back. This results in a fuller, more productive plant. But at some point, we need to stop pinching back or the plant will remain stunted and produce very little.

In the same way, behaviors that likely encourage growth in a young company can compromise its growth later in life. Through my observations of hundreds of business owners and managers that are captured in this book, I believe that you will be better able to identify these behaviors in yourself and in those around you. With that awareness, you will be better prepared to manage and modify these behaviors and, in doing so, build stronger, long-term success for your organization as well as increased personal satisfaction and happiness for yourself, your employees, and your family.

CHAPTER I

BEHAVE YOURSELF

Groundhog Day

Running a small business can sometimes feel like being caught up in the movie *Groundhog Day*, the 1993 comedy starring Bill Murray, Andie MacDowell, and Chris Elliott. In the movie, egocentric TV weatherman Phil Connors, played by Murray, is stuck in Punxsutawney, Pennsylvania on Groundhog Day due to a snowstorm. The movie follows Connors as he relives the same day over and over again for an undetermined, but very long, period of time.

The message is unstated, but we are led to believe his self-absorbed behavior may be to blame for the situation Connors finds himself in. He's been given the chance to observe his faults and correct them. It's only with the help of TV producer Rita (MacDowell) that Connors is eventually led to an understanding of his rude and insensitive behavior and finally wakes up on February 3, a chastened and better person.

Groundhog Day is a funny movie worth watching, but I must admit it would be even funnier if it didn't strike so close to home. The idea of reliving the same day over and over, of making the same mistakes time and time again, sounds so much like life inside some small businesses.

There are lots of reasons small businesses stay that way. Some are kept small intentionally by owners who elect to keep the business an intimate size that fits their personal style. Some are constrained by technical limitations, market pressures, financing options, or competitive concerns. But far too often, owners who would very much like to grow their business unintentionally keep their company small by entrepreneurial behaviors that derail potential growth.

Executive coach and author Marshall Goldsmith hits the nail on the head when he states, "The higher you go [in business] the more your problems are behavioral." The extent to which we can master our behaviors will have a profound effect on the success of our organization. When we fail to master our behaviors, or surround ourselves with people who exhibit them, we find ourselves repeating the same mistakes and reliving the same consequences. Welcome to *Groundhog Day!*

Connors was blind to his own shortcomings. He was disliked and distrusted by others but completely disinterested in what others thought or felt about him. As a result, he was held back from advancement, trapped in a job he didn't like, and doing things he didn't enjoy, including covering non-news stories like the annual Groundhog Day event. Coworkers, hoping to guide him to more positive and productive behaviors, pointed out opportunities to make changes, but their words fell on deaf ears.

It wasn't until Connors entered the loop of recurring Groundhog Days that he began to understand how his own behaviors were conspiring against him. Once he gained that awareness, he was able to modify his actions in positive ways, leading to greater happiness and, in the end, getting the girl.

As business leaders, we need to be aware of our behaviors and recognize how they may be conspiring against us. And, like Connors, we need to use that awareness as an opportunity to modify or channel our behaviors in ways that will enable us to achieve more productive outcomes. When we do so, we can move on to a better future for our business.

Behavior Modification

No doubt you've heard the saying about how important it is to stop working IN your business and start working ON your business. That's good advice, but I don't feel it goes far enough. Considering how tightly business performance is tied to the owner's behavior, it may be more important for the owner to focus their attention toward working on themselves.

You may be thinking, "Why should I worry about my behaviors? This is just the way I am, and it seems to have worked great up to this point." If you don't go any further than this chapter, it will no doubt be because you are unable to see any fault in your behaviors. That would be unfortunate, because almost every entrepreneur exhibits one or more of the behaviors in this book, to the detriment of their organization.

For those who do finish the book, it will be clear that you have an open mind. You are able to take a crucial first step, a step back, and make a critical assessment of the way you behave. Congratulations if you do, because it can be very hard to question the personal behaviors that are so central to who we are.

True, our behaviors got us to where we are today, so there is (or at least there was) considerable value in them. But, as Goldsmith points out in his book, the things that got us where we are today may not be enough to get us where we want to go.

The six behaviors that comprise the Entrepreneurial Conspiracy have nothing to do with the behaviors that are carefully assessed, cataloged, and analyzed in personality assessments such as DiSC, Myers-Briggs Type Indicator, Keirsey Temperament Sorter, or others. In the hands of trained evaluators, these assessments provide detailed insights into who we are, why we behave the way we do, and how we interact with others.

Some dismiss those assessments as touchy-feely mumbo jumbo, but their broad use shows that many people put considerable stock in their results. The self-awareness gathered from these types of assessments provides guidance for:

- Improved communication
- More effective change initiatives
- More productive teams
- Increased ability to motivate others
- Reduced conflict
- More profitable sales conversations
- Greater cooperation

With the six behaviors of the Entrepreneurial Conspiracy, there is no paper-and-pencil test or online tool to help identify them. They were discovered through my working with small business owners and by looking at myself in the mirror and realizing what was affecting my own businesses' performance.

This book will help you identify, assess, and correct any of these behaviors that you see in yourself. This may be difficult. Just as we don't consciously think about making our heart beat or our lungs expand and contract, we don't think about our behaviors. It is simply the way we are. But to successfully change these behaviors starts with recognizing they are there.

I will point out specific signs and symptoms that should help identify the behaviors, but this still involves a self-awareness that many people lack. We are simply not inclined to see faults in ourselves. If you reach the end of this book and say to yourself, "That was a complete waste of time, because none of that applied to me," then you might want to share some of the concepts with your employees or spouse to see if they agree with your self-assessment. My bet is that their view from the outside may not exactly match your view from the inside.

Early on in my experience working with entrepreneurs it became clear that the business results they achieved were heavily influenced by the behaviors they brought to their company. Trying to improve the performance of a company by addressing only the technical elements such as competitive position, operating efficiencies, quality, or profitability without addressing the owner's behavior only produced short-term results. Ultimately, the behaviors will win out and can undermine or undo any technical improvements.

I am not suggesting for a minute that you change who you are. No doubt you are a warm, caring, and generally nice person. But I am equally confident that some of your behaviors are less than productive when it comes to the success of your business.[1]

It is a tenet of supervision that we shouldn't manage people based on what we believe they are thinking or feeling. Instead, we should manage their behavior. In providing feedback to an employee, it's usually not a good idea to tell them something like, "You seem angry." It's very likely we could have misinterpreted what we thought we saw and end up aggravating the situation.

Instead, good supervisory technique suggests that we address exactly what we can see. Rather than saying, "You seem angry," we would say, "I noticed you raising your voice, shouting, and pounding on the conference table," and let them fill in the blanks about why they were behaving that way. We may eventually want to identify and correct what's driving their behavior, but when it comes down to it, we don't really need to concern ourself with what the person feels. We need them to manage their negative feelings and express them in a way that maintains a positive working environment.

The same holds true for you. Focus on correcting any of the six behaviors that apply to you. While doing so, it may feel uncomfortable, like you aren't being true to your authentic self; that the changes really don't reflect the true you. Instead, they'll feel like a pair of pants that don't quite fit. But if you are sincerely interested in enhancing your prospects for long-term profitability, then you will no doubt find that the changes begin to fit you very nicely. The internal you will become quite comfortable with your new external behaviors, to the benefit of your employees, customers, suppliers and, ultimately, to your business.

Hurdling the Barriers to Change

When it comes to the things that are most frightening in business, there's still a lot of the six-year-old in each of us. Hearing the noise under the bed or walking into a dark room can give a kid the trembles. Business owners are also most frightened of the dangers and adversaries we can't see, which includes our own behaviors.

We can't see or touch them. We can't measure them or track them in a spreadsheet or on a graph. We can't apply metrics or key performance indicators (KPIs) to them. That's why entrepreneurs tend to focus our attention on solving the more-tangible issues we face. In business, owners are especially comfortable dealing with operational issues. The early days of business were mainly spent figuring out how to get the job done, so unraveling these kinds of problems is downright enjoyable. As our business grows, we develop increasing comfort and familiarity with the challenges of dealing with equipment, customers, and workers. Again, these are visible challenges.

Dealing with behaviors, on the other hand—especially our own—is something we'd prefer to avoid or ignore.

Another barrier to behavior modification is a simple lack of awareness. It's tough to recognize our own bad behaviors, because unless we're willing to be video recorded throughout the day, we can't see the way we act. How we discover that our behaviors are a problem is by the reaction or response they get. This awareness of how our behaviors affect others, and therefore our business, is something that comes naturally to only a few.

It requires effort, sometimes tremendous effort, to be attentive to how others respond to our behavior. We tend to say or do something, get a nod of understanding, assume things are good, and then we are off to the next thing. But to determine the true response, we need to crank up our interpersonal antenna and spend a moment tuning it. Did they really just accept and agree with the behavior? How did they actually interpret it and internally respond?

North American business people traveling to China have consistently been surprised and disappointed by the failure of their Asian business partners to follow through on agreements. A meeting is held, actions are discussed, heads nod, and we return to America expecting those actions will happen. Often they don't.

The reason is that, in China, nodding and smiling doesn't mean "I agree," it simply means "I hear you." We misinterpret their apparent agreement and are disappointed when those agreements aren't honored.

When our employees, customers, and suppliers nod in agreement, we need to confirm that they actually agree. Do they think our behavior is the right or best approach, or is nodding simply their way of completing the interaction as quickly as possible? We must not assume our behavior got the desired reaction and is, in fact, best for the long-term success of our business just because people didn't challenge us on it.

One of the truly frustrating parts about communicating with others is that we need to consider how the person observing our behavior or interacting with us will interpret what we've done or said. Almost everyone has experienced an exchange like this:

"Don't take that tone with me!"

"What tone? I didn't take any tone!"

There's a good chance there was no tone intended, but the person we were speaking to heard tone. How is this possible? It's because we modify and adapt everything we see and hear through our own constantly shifting set of filters.

Does the person we're talking with have some past experience that colors their reaction to what we say and do? Do they fundamentally not trust us for some reason? Did their cat throw up on their brand-new couch this morning? Any of these things and a thousand more can change someone's perceptions of our words and actions. We need to turn up our antenna, pay attention to any clues we can decipher, and try to assess their true reaction to our words and actions.

And if our antenna is a bit rusty, or if we want to be absolutely certain of someone's response, we can take a more direct approach and simply ask, "What do you think?" When taking this approach, our tone is truly important. If the person senses we really are interested in their response, and we have the kind of relationship that makes them comfortable being frank with us, then we will get Grade A, prime-cut, all-natural and actionable feedback. This gives us a crystal clear picture of how people are responding to our behavior and their beliefs about how it is affecting our business, whether in a positive or negative way.

On the other hand, if they sense we're just going through the motions, that we know we're expected to ask for feedback so we thought we'd give it a shot, then we shouldn't expect to actually learn anything from their response. We will have just taken a step backwards in building credibility and trust, and exhibited yet another bad entrepreneurial behavior.

Fix the Roof

Anyone who's been involved in a Lean initiative or an organized process-improvement effort knows that it's critical to start with a big-picture view. We need to see how all the pieces fit together before we start trying to fix any of the individual problems. Otherwise, improvements we make here could cause problems there.

In manufacturing, a tremendous way to reduce costs is to minimize finished inventory. Cut inventory and we cut carrying costs and can also reduce overhead by eliminating warehouse space and staff. But we could end up with very unhappy customers if the speedy delivery they had when we went to the warehouse to fill their order is replaced by a six-week backorder, waiting for the product to be produced.

It's better to look at inventory in a more holistic way. What are the factors that drive inventory levels? Is there some trigger or process upstream that, if addressed, would resolve the issue while not disappointing customers?

In our business, we could probably put our finger on a number of functions or performance measures that could be improved. Some of them may be in desperate need of improvement. But before jumping and fixing the wrong thing, we need to step back and take that big-picture view. The fundamental fact is that many of the problems small businesses face are really symptoms or results of the management behaviors that owners bring to their business. In research conducted for their book, *The Founder's Mentality*, authors Chris Zook and James Allen found that with large organizations, internal factors are five times more likely to impact profitable growth than outside factors. In small businesses, this is magnified by the dominant role most owners play in them. And, it's complicated even further by owners who exhibit counterproductive behaviors.

Addressing a business problem without addressing the behavior that causes it is like trying to fix a leaky roof by placing pans inside the house to catch the rain. Any improvement we get is temporary. The cause of the problem is still there and will show itself again the next time it rains. And the leak in the roof is likely to spread, creating a bigger problem. If we fail to address bad behaviors causing issues in our business, the best we can hope for is that our business becomes an unpleasant place to work. The worst case scenario is that the metaphorical roof collapses.

The behaviors I address in this book exist in businesses of all sizes, from startups and solo operations (which might explain why so many businesses remain solo operations) to multi-million-dollar enterprises. They also exist at all levels of management; they just appear more pronounced among a company's ownership or upper management level.

These behaviors can be, and frequently are, strengths at some point in the life cycle of our business, but unless recognized and addressed, they will certainly become weaknesses as the company grows.

Rarely does one of the behaviors stand alone. More often than not, the presence of one behavior signals or results in the presence of another. And each behavior is highly contagious. While they originate with the owner, they are readily spread throughout an organization. The behaviors work together silently, insidiously, and relentlessly. They collude to undermine our efforts, usurp our authority, and undo our vision. These six behaviors are co-conspirators in the Entrepreneurial Conspiracy.

CHAPTER 2
BLURRED VISION

Symptoms

For leadership, employees typically turn to the person who owns or manages the business. This may include the routine, logistical details of who should do what when, but taking care of details like this is really management rather than leadership. Anyone skilled in organization can provide that kind of direction, so it shouldn't necessarily fall to the owner if there are managers in the business.

When we talk about leadership, we also aren't talking about making sure that operational tasks are being performed. That's supervision.

Leadership addresses the bigger picture. As a leader, we are defining our goals for the business and the roles we expect our employees to play in reaching those goals. What personality do we want the company to present to our customers and the community? What values do we want our company to represent? These are the aspects of leadership that can't come from an operations manager. They must come from the owner.

Those and a hundred more facets of business are things we must share with our employees and possibly with our customers and suppliers as well. But before we can share them, we need to form a crystal clear picture of them for ourself. Doing this requires soul searching about our expectations of, and hopes for, the business.

A hard look at how the business is performing is also required. What are the strengths or positives that are propelling future growth? What are the weaknesses or negatives that are holding it back? Only after working this all out for ourself, and forming a vision for our organization, can we share that vision with others and fulfill our role as the leader.

The first behavior in The Entrepreneurial Conspiracy prevents the owner and the organization from seeing those things. We refer to this behavior as Blurred Vision, and it can be recognized in this client's story.

Alphonse's Amazing Cleaning Company[2] enjoyed several years of aggressive growth, strong profitability, and healthy cash flow. Alphonse had managed to grow the company from $1.5 million to $7 million in annual revenue in just four years. His crews worked day and night handling all the work that flooded in. While it took considerable energy and determination, they maintained the high level of quality their customers demanded, put out the frequent operations fires that are common in fast-growth companies, and staffed frontline and management positions as the business continued to grow.

The company's strong CFO kept them always operating from a budget, but the rest of the strategic plan was weak and gave little attention to sales and marketing, organizational health, or operations. Furthermore, the plan was held close to the vest by Alphonse, the owner/CEO.

Alphonse was an engaging guy with unquestioned integrity. He was the kind of person everyone likes, earning the respect and loyalty of those he encountered. He was always available to talk with employees and suppliers. But as the company grew and Alphonse began to add managers to handle the different business divisions, he found himself increasingly removed from daily, direct contact with most of his people. He no longer had a regular opportunity to personally share his vision for the company through casual conversations.

He had given his business strategy a lot of thought and had a fairly clear course of action mapped out. But the strategy and plan existed only in his head, and he was reluctant to commit it to paper and share it with others. Without a shared vision of where the company was headed and what the employees' roles were, it was impossible to assign any accountability. No one knew exactly what their job was or how their performance was being evaluated.

Instead, everyone worked from Alphonse's daily to-do lists and extinguished the fires that sprang up in their area. The division managers worked on their own agenda with little regard for the needs or agendas of other divisions. There was no common, long-term goal, no "flag on the hill" that everyone could see and work together to achieve.

Absent a common objective and clear accountabilities, the efforts of the managers and employees were uncoordinated, ineffective, and sometimes at cross-purposes; what one division manager did undermined the success of other divisions.

Due to the company's blurred vision, it got off course, went into a stall, and would no doubt have crashed and burned. Fortunately, Alphonse realized that he'd done a poor job of helping the people around him understand his vision for the company. With some outside help, he developed a formal vision statement as part of a strategic plan for his business and shared it with the employees who would be tasked with making it happen.

Because Alphonse recognized the problem in time and was able to address it, things turned around in his company.

....

This story includes the fact that Alphonse was reluctant to share his vision for the company with others. Why would a business owner NOT want to share the very thing that describes where the organization is heading, including the strategy to follow to reach its goals?

Part of the reluctance could be a lack of knowledge about how to share. Good communication skills typically aren't a strong suit of many entrepreneurs. The fact is, performing the day-to-day tasks in our job can be a fairly solitary activity in any business, and frequently that's a necessary part of launching one. Many owners of growing companies just don't know how to go about socializing[3] their vision and strategy.

A large number of entrepreneurs, if we are being honest with ourselves, would admit that we really don't want to share such information. We tend to play our cards close to the vest. Sharing our vision for the business would mean throwing down our cards for everyone to see, and that's something that makes us uncomfortable.

We may not want to show our cards because our hand is weak. We worry that if our employees knew how dicey things were, they'd look for work somewhere else. If our banker knew how shaky things were, they'd stop lending us money. And if our spouse knew, they'd make us fold up our tent and go get a real job.

And that connects to yet another reason for our reluctance—the fear of being found out. This is what psychologists refer to as "imposter syndrome," where a person has an internalized fear of being exposed as a fraud.

Most entrepreneurs have a passion for their vision, but not all of us have the firm confidence that it makes sense. As long as the vision lives only in our head, we can bluff our way through the day-to-day operations, and employees have no recourse but to assume we know what we are doing. With that knowledge safely stored in our prefrontal cortex, employees trust that we have a solid plan for success. But when the vision is published and out there for everyone to see, we worry it won't hold up to scrutiny, and that it will get questioned, maybe even challenged, by the people reading it. Asked to explain, clarify, and justify the vision, some owners are afraid we will be exposed as not being the smartest person in the room, a position we are often loathe to relinquish. Or we may simply resent the idea of employees passing any sort of judgement on our vision for the company's future.

When we, as owners, fail to tell employees where we see the company headed, the entire organization suffers from Blurred Vision.

Indications of Blurred Vision

One of the great conundrums of my youth was how to look up the spelling of a word in the dictionary. This was a classic Catch 22[4] because looking up the word requires that you know how to spell it.

That's much less of a problem today, as the internet has largely eliminated this, along with the need for paper dictionaries. Type "spell" along with even the most mangled version of the word into a search engine, and those wily algorithms will almost certainly reply with "did you mean ..." along with the correct spelling of the word.

One of the conundrums of Blurred Vision is that it helps to have clear vision to recognize whether or not you have Blurred Vision. Fortunately, there are a few obvious indicators that even the blurriest of business owners should be able to identify.

One is repeatedly latching onto the latest, best thing. We attend a seminar or read a book about the latest and greatest way to propel our business into the land of unimaginable profit. Then we excitedly gather our team, tell them about the new recipe for success, and give them a list of the things they need to do to make it a reality.

Everyone is duly impressed, salutes smartly, and does their best to implement the items on the list. Undoubtedly some of the things will create improvements, while others are less effective. No matter, because not so very long after that list is issued, we go to another seminar, read another book, or just get up one morning and come up with a new and even better list!

Unsure about the reason for the shift in direction, some brave employee will raise a hand and ask what was wrong with the first list, why is the new list better, and should they now try to follow both lists.

"Don't worry about the old list, just do what's on the new list," is our reply.

You can imagine the reaction from the team. Confusion regarding what to do. Exhaustion from trying to constantly adapt to the latest list. Frustration at the wasted effort and energy. They feel like they are trapped on an airplane that constantly changes course and never gets to its destination.

While it's essential to regularly fine-tune and adjust the course of our business, these adjustments should be made based on well-considered revisions to our company's strategy or significant shifts in the market. Affixing ourself to the business fad-of-the-day isn't leadership. It's a clear sign of Blurred Vision.

The Beneficial Early Blur

For young organizations, the lack of a vision may not be a problem and could actually be a strength. That's because things are very fluid in the early days of a business. Most fresh, young entrepreneurs really don't have a clear idea of what they want their business to look like in five or more years, and that's okay.

Some of us may have entered our industry after deciding that the services we would deliver or the products we would produce and sell would be something we could do well and make a living at. We may not have fully understood the many forms our business could take or what niche it would fill. Everything is a blur in the beginning, and we often are literally making it up as we go along. There's no sense spending time crafting a vision when it is going to change on a daily basis. Besides, it's just us! There's no one to share the vision with yet.

Others may have been in the business as the employee of a similar company. Whether we left because of personality issues with the owner, discomfort about the way the business was run, or because we had an idea for how to do it better, we struck out on our own. In this case, we are likely to be laser-focused on improving the thing or things that so disappointed or angered us at our previous job. If we have any employees, the only aspect of our vision that we are likely to share is what we want done differently from the company we left.

Regardless of how or why new businesses come into being, it's probably good that we keep our vision a bit unfocused. Doing so helps us be nimble and flexible. Our lack of focus helps us be alert to opportunities we might otherwise miss.[5] As we discover our internal strengths and recognize external opportunities, a vision will begin to come into focus. But developing and committing to a vision too early in the life of a business could result in a stratified plan that won't work.

I live in a small, older lake community in northeast Ohio. Many of the houses here began as fishing or summer cottages that have been repeatedly added onto and expanded. Unfortunately, the shape and contour of the lots prevent many of my neighbors from having an attached garage. On cold winter mornings, neighbors can often be seen driving our narrow, hilly roads with only the smallest window of visibility through their front windshield. They look like some Inuit version of a tank driver, maneuvering their snow-covered vehicles with limited forward vision and none to the rear or sides. Clearly, they are putting not only themselves at risk, but anyone else who approaches from outside their tight range of sight.

Every business owner launches their business in the hopes that they will be able to keep it on the road to success. But owners who lack a clear perspective of where they are headed, along with the peripheral vision that comes from awareness and consideration of opportunities and obstacles they must negotiate, are similarly at risk.

As my neighbors head out on snowy mornings, they are reasonably safe for the first part of their trip. In our neighborhood there's no cross traffic, few pedestrians, and the speed limit is only 15 mph. But once they get to the highway, all manner of mayhem could be around the next turn.

Similarly, as a new business starts its journey to success, Blurred Vision isn't likely to be a problem. But as we settle on a course, build speed, and take on more passengers—employees and family members who rely on us and the business—clarity of vision becomes essential. Every day that we fail to form and share a vision for the company is another day we put our company at risk of crashing and burning.

Causes

As entrepreneurs, we have the deck stacked against us when it comes to providing clear vision. In the early days of our business, the emphasis is on survival and winning some quick successes. Our vision sometimes doesn't extend beyond meeting the next payroll. Given this situation, it would be pointless to focus on business planning that extends beyond the next 12 months. In some cases, a company's long-range plan means making it to the next payroll!

As if those distractions weren't enough to blur our focus, a lot of entrepreneurs seem to be genetically hardwired with a case of what I call Entrepreneurial Drift, or

E-Drift. That's the short attention span and easily distracted personality character-istics many of us bring to our company. E-Drift is another one of the six behaviors, and I explore it in greater detail in Chapter 5.

For now, let me mention that E-Drift isn't all bad. After all, it may have been this very characteristic that led us to start our business in the first place. It's the constant, nagging dissatisfaction with the status quo; that endless need to tweak things to make them better; the restlessness inside that compels us to explore new things.

However, too often our E-Drift can run wild. It becomes the destructive version of the same creative energy and unbridled force that originally caused us to launch our business. It can leave us distracted, focused on too many things, and, as a result, focused on nothing. It's when we don't rein that energy in, harness it, and give it a positive direction that it dilutes our focus and undermines the growth of our company.

The opposite of E-Drift is focus, which is the ability for us and our executive team to home in on the handful of key priorities that must be addressed in order to success-fully grow the company. The Law of Focus states that no element in the universe is as powerful when dispersed as it is when focused. When focused, the energy, intelli-gence, and innovation of the team is a force for profitable growth.

Once achieved, that focus requires continued concentration to maintain ... not for a day, a week, or even a month, but for as long as we continue to lead our business or advise those who do.

Sustained, sharp focus is what Jim Collins writes about in his book, *Good to Great*, when he describes The Hedgehog Concept. Given the choice between being a fox or a hedgehog, most would choose to be a fox. This makes sense, because foxes are sleek, intelligent, and beautiful animals that are often written about in stories and fairy tales. Hedgehogs, on the other hand, are small, ordinary creatures notable only because they are covered with spines, similar to porcupines. How many stories do you know of about hedgehogs? Likely, this is the first.

What makes the hedgehog a more appropriate model for business behavior is summarized in the ancient Greek saying, "The fox knows many things, but the hedgehog knows one big thing." Hedgehogs are slow, steady, unassuming, and singu-larly focused on getting safely through the day. Based on longevity, the hedgehog seems to be superior to the fox that is likely to end up draped around the neck of a well-to-do woman or hunted down by a pack of barking beagles and oddly dressed guys on horseback. As for me, I'll take the hedgehog.

Bright Shiny Things

Besides the dangers of simply losing focus, there's also the problem of focusing on the wrong things. It's like being distracted by interesting sights as we drive, rather than keeping our focus on the road ahead. Absent a clear, shared vision of where our business is headed in the long run, we will be tempted to take detours from our planned route, most likely wasting time and often winding up at a dead end.

Maybe we should expand our market into a new geographic territory. Or how about adding some lines or services unrelated to what we currently have that might bring in new business? The list of possible detours and distractions is endless. They may be fine ideas with tremendous potential, but are they within the boundaries of the vision we've set for the company? Are these ideas or opportunities aligned with our long-term goals? If not, then we need to keep our eyes on the road and follow the course we've set, rather than letting our vision be blurred by the next bright, shiny thing that pops up along the way.

When our vision gets blurred and we start unexpectedly changing direction, we will confuse everyone in our organization. And if we have shared our vision for the company, but then suddenly start to steer off the planned course, employees can't help but be confused. They'll become uncertain about what they are supposed to be doing and may start working at cross purposes. Unsure of whether they are working on the right things and going in the right direction, they will become frustrated, de-energized, and disengaged.

This doesn't mean our people won't be working hard or don't care. Just the opposite could be true; they will redouble their efforts. That makes their activity all the more frustrating and exhausting for them. Unless our vision refocuses, they are likely to ask us to pull over and let them out of the car.

I'm certainly not implying that we should never adjust course. Things change, and they can sometimes change fast, requiring an instant shift of direction. Every smart business owner knows, sometimes we need to "call an audible" when we see that the current direction is misguided or there's an obstacle ahead. No time for a sit-down with the team. We need to act now!

This sense of urgency is seldom appropriate, though. In most cases, if we're going to deviate from our set course, it should be done with thought and deliberation. This ensures that the change makes sense and isn't a spontaneous, and possibly inappropriate, response to the situation. One that we will later regret.

There will always be new opportunities or ideas that come along. It may make perfect sense to pursue them, but not with a sudden jerk of the steering wheel that takes the company off course and into unknown territory. There's almost always time to give careful, measured consideration; to overlay new opportunities on top of the vision and see if they're in alignment. If not, is the opportunity so loaded with potential that perhaps it merits reconsidering the vision? If the decision is made to refocus the vision to bring it into alignment with the new opportunity, we should do so only after performing due diligence and having a clear focus on the ramifications for the organization and its long-term direction. Not simply because it feels right in that moment.

When we are constantly changing direction, our employees, customers, and suppliers quickly become confused. They lose the guideposts that were keeping them on course. When this happens, nobody in the organization knows where the company is headed next. Employees don't have a chance to produce the results the company needs, so the company never gains traction on achieving its goals, even when those goals are things as fundamental as delivering consistent quality, retaining good employees, or achieving healthy cash flow.

Some zigzagging on vision isn't really related to our visition being blurred, but to another behavioral characteristic that pits what's in our head against what's in our heart. At some point in our life, most of us struggle with the conflict between what we say we want to do or have (what's in our head), and what we actually believe, deep down, we're capable of doing or worthy of having (what's in our heart).

This conflict is described in the book *The Fifth Discipline* by Harvard professor Peter Senge. The book refers to this situation as a Structural Conflict. I saw this conflict play out with my clients for years, and I experienced it in my own business before I knew there was a name for it. Clients would get very close to achieving a long-held goal only to come up short at the last minute. They seemed to hit an inner brick wall as they moved closer to achieving the things they wanted.

Senge explains how this loss of drive toward achieving the vision is rooted in one of two beliefs. First is the belief that we are powerless to bring about the things we really care about. The second, and less common, belief is that we are unworthy and don't deserve to have the things we truly desire. Both beliefs stand in the way of achieving our vision.

In the book, rather than describing the difficulty as hitting a wall, the author used the analogy of being caught between two rubber bands. Imagine you are standing between two sturdy posts, one to either side of you, 15 feet away. Around your waist are two very large rubber bands, one attached to the post on your right (your vision) and the other attached to the post on your left (your beliefs). As you strive to reach the vision that is in your heart, the closer you get, the more tension there is from the opposing force created by the beliefs that are held in your head. So the closer you get to achieving your vision, the stronger the pull-back force becomes.

What's in our head manifests as negative self-talk. Our doubts build, momentum wanes, and we are pulled in the other direction rather than continuing to push on and achieve our vision. To others, the change in direction appears to be the same as a common symptom of Blurred Vision would be. In fact, it's a different impediment to progress that may need to be addressed.

Senge says that one of these two belief systems is at work in almost everyone. At first, I found this discouraging, but I've learned that being armed with awareness of this conflict between head and heart allows me to better prepare to shut down the doubts and negative self-talk and realize my vision. This is something that can be overcome, but not if we are blind to it.

Vision Statement? Who Has Time?!

During my work with business owners, I've discovered that the times when they and their companies are least at risk of failure is during the startup phase or when experiencing financial difficulty. While on the surface this might seem counterintuitive, it makes a lot of sense when looking more closely, and it has to do with the focus of the owner.

In those heady, early days when our company was still shiny and new, our enthusiasm and passion were limitless. Whether we'd finally realized a lifelong dream to be self-employed, or were driven by outside forces to jump into the entrepreneurial pool, it was a thrilling time. We were the master of our own fate, and every day brought fresh, exciting challenges. We could almost smell the adrenaline as we addressed the seemingly unending list of things that had to be done.

If we'd been given such a list while working for someone else, no doubt we would have thrown up our hands in desperation, thought to ourself that it couldn't be done, and probably cursed our boss for setting impossible expectations. But it's different when it's our list for our own business. Every time we checked another thing off the list, we moved ourself closer to being a profitable entrepreneur.

Most of us didn't have a written vision or mission, but there was no need for them. We knew exactly what they were! And if someone else needed to know, we could personally share our vision and mission with them while ensuring they were on board. After all, at that stage, they could probably have been condensed to just a few words: survive, grow, make money.

For companies past the survival stage and looking ahead to the growth stage, financial trouble might seem to be a major threat to the business. But this is probably not so. After all, if you want to gain the total attention of an entrepreneur, just mess with their money! When financial problems turn up on an entrepreneur's radar, we will focus all our time, energy, and talent to solve the problem and remove the threat.

Focus is what enables entrepreneurs to overcome these threats to our business. But as the business begins to enjoy success, we sometimes lose that focus. It's a bit of a paradigm shift; when things are going along absolutely great is when entrepreneurs can be most at risk. It's similar to what happens when the front end of our car is out of alignment.

At lower speeds we probably won't even notice anything, except maybe a slight tendency of the car to drift one way or another. But once we get it out on the highway, the problem becomes much more obvious and dangerous. The car will have a strong tendency to head into the median or oncoming traffic, neither of which is likely to turn out well for us as the driver.

If our business is coasting along, things remain pretty much status quo, and if there's slow or no growth, we aren't going to sense a lack of focus. As our company makes minor drifts left or right, they are easy to detect and simple to correct. As our business accelerates, the drifts are faster, more pronounced, and harder to correct. Unless we are sharply focused on the business, we could drive it right into a ditch.

Consequences

I already described the confusion and frustration that results when operating a business with no clearly defined course due to a blurred vision.

Customers may be confused about how we fit into their list of service providers. If we branch into too many new services or markets, if we change our selling proposition, current customers may wonder if we will continue to provide them the same services they relied on us to provide in the past or if they will need to find a new supplier.

Customers may also be confused about the nature or character of the company. Some people make their buying decisions based strictly on price. They aren't interested in building a relationship with a trusted service provider. Fortunately, there are probably far more customers out there who prefer to work with suppliers they know and who know them. Those customers want to have confidence in the people with whom they do business. These are the loyal, high-value customers who return again and again, building a reliable revenue stream.

When blurred vision results in frequent and possibly confusing shifts in the character of a business, customers will also be confused. Are we really the same company they've relied on in the past, or is the company going in some new direction?

Customers are greatly impressed and reassured when they see the same workers on their premises or when they deal with the same people in the office. Unfortunately, a blurred vision makes it more likely that customers will seldom see the same people more than once or twice.

That's because employees working in a company that lacks clear vision are likely to burn out. It is exhausting for them to deal with not knowing what's expected of them, or, just as bad, to deal with an ever-changing list of expectations. Eventually, they will have had enough and take their skills elsewhere, to a company that knows where it's headed. They may even decide to strike out and create their own company—one with a clear vision.

Blurred Vision conspires with other behavioral issues, including No Accountability, Heroic Management, and as I mentioned earlier, E-Drift.

No Accountability is created when the goals of the business aren't written down and shared with others, making it impossible to hold us, as the owner, accountable for meeting those goals. When no one knows the planned destination, neither us nor our employees can tell if we are on course to getting there.

A friend of mine told me about how, when he was young, his father would often take "the scenic route." At random times while the family was in the car, his father would—apparently on a whim—depart from the route to their planned destination. The family might spend the next hour or two meandering around back streets or country roads. It was never apparent if his father was actually trying to find something or he just wanted to wander. Eventually, he would find his way back to a road that put them on course to their original destination.

My friend, his brother, and their mother failed to find much joy in these diversions. It's not like they saw anything particularly interesting or were pleasantly surprised beneficiaries of an unannounced stop at an ice cream stand. They were unwilling ride-alongs who would have much preferred to have stayed on course or at least have been informed of the purpose for the extra miles tacked on to their trip.

In a business driven by someone with Blurred Vision, it's pointless to ask "Are we there yet?" because the owner doesn't know where they're going. That's No Accountability.

Blurred Vision spawns Heroic Management because the owner gets to be the smartest person in the room. Team members can't help solve problems, because they can't be sure what the problems are or the appropriate way to fix them. Only the owner has, or pretends to have, a clear picture of the situation and, therefore, only they can resolve it.

Engaging our team in resolving problems and identifying new opportunities is essential to achieving the highest possible levels of performance in our company. But as a Heroic Manager, we shoulder all that responsibility and leave team members uncomfortable about what's going to happen next.

Blurred Vision is both affected by and plays into the owner's E-Drift. Because the plan has not been formalized in writing, the owner is free to chase the next shiny object and then claim it as the vision du jour.

Solutions

Capture the Flag

In addition to organized sports, my kids had plenty of homegrown games they would play in our neighborhood. A favorite was Capture the Flag. This is a pretty simple game with few rules and only two pieces of equipment—something designated as a flag for each of the two teams. Of course they weren't really flags; more likely they were old dish towels nabbed from our kitchen or from the rag bag. Each team hid their flag, and it was game on as the opposing team tried to find it.

Naturally, it was essential that all players knew exactly what the flag they were searching for looked like. Without that critical piece of information, the players would have no idea if they found the flag. The fun of the game would have instantly turned into the frustration of confused efforts to pursue an unclear goal. How many kids would want to be picked for our team if we didn't, or couldn't, tell them what their objective was? My guess is not many.

It's no different in business, especially when working with competitive employees who want to play an active part in the game and who want to win. They may not want or need to be the leader of the team, but they need to understand what goal they are all working toward. When our people ask us where the company is headed or why we're making some of the decisions we're making, most aren't challenging our authority. They just want to contribute all they can to the team's victory.

But in too many small businesses, the only person who has a really clear picture of the flag they're trying to capture is the owner. And the place where this closely guarded picture lives is often between the owner's ears. Just as in the childhood game, when those in our company can see the flag, measure it, and understand their role in capturing it, the game becomes much easier to win and a lot more fun to play. When we encourage our people, especially our key people, to have a voice in defining the flag and the strategy to capture it, we have an even better chance of winning.

Smart business owners surround themselves with good, smart, energized people. That can be uncomfortable for many owners because we no longer get to be the smartest person in the room. We have to admit to the team that someone else might have a better idea. When an employee asks, "Are you sure that's the right choice?" or suggests an alternate option to the one we proposed, at first it can feel like insubordination or downright defiance.

Get over it. We don't need to have all the answers or provide all the energy to move our organization forward. We need to accept that there are other people who know more than we do and that other perspectives are as good or better than ours. Remember that it's still our business and will be for as long as we want to hold on to it. But for as long as we're at the helm, we will need an outstanding crew if we're going to achieve maximum speed and keep the business in top shape.

Why, Where, and How

When we lack a crystal clear picture of just what business we're in and where it's headed, the business is doomed to flounder and fail while we and our employees suffer the consequences. But how do we take all that brilliance that's bumping around inside our brain and convert it into something that's coherent and can be shared with others? A friend of mine, when faced with any enormous task, approaches it with calmness. He says it's like eating an elephant—you do it one bite at a time.

To begin to eat the elephant of capturing our thoughts about our business, we're going to break it down into three courses:

- Define WHY we're in business in the first place,
- Decide WHERE we're trying to go, and
- Determine HOW to get there.

Let's start with the Why.

Small businesses are outward expressions of the values and beliefs of their owners. To make this concept a little more concrete, let's think of our business as a tree. The tree has a trunk, branches, and leaves. All these are visible to people who look at it. But there's a part of the tree that people don't see—the roots. And it's the roots that determine the size and shape of the part of the tree that can be seen.

For a small business, the roots are our values and beliefs. It's our essence. It's what makes us the unique human and extraordinary businessperson we are ... or hope to be. Just as with a tree, the root structure is the core from which everything about us grows. We need to look here for the Why of our business.

This is a good time to go deep. We should start with considering what it is that we want out of life. Why are we here on this earth? What is our purpose? When it comes time to leave this life, what is it that we want to be remembered for or leave behind? A lot of entrepreneurs find that the answers to these questions are tightly intertwined with the answers to questions about why we started our business in the first place.

So why DID we start our business? What was it that motivated us to make that huge leap and become an entrepreneur? It was a frightening step, full of risk and potential for failure. So why did we do it?

As we contemplate and write the answer to this question, we need to make sure it's our idea and not someone else's. It's easy to get caught up in what other companies are doing or in inventing a lofty reason that doesn't ring true. The result is that we never really understand it ourselves. We need to speak from our own heart and use our own words.

If we can't articulate and write down our Why, then we're in trouble from the get-go. Without a clear Why, we are going to have trouble with the Where and the How. This can be seen every day in business owners who talk about wanting to build a big business with lots of trucks on the road and pockets full of money. But they never seem to get beyond doing the work themselves. Or the owner who does succeed in building a big company, but discovers once they have it that it really isn't what they wanted in the first place, so they sell it or shrink the company back to a size they're comfortable owning and running.

With answers to Why, we're now working from a solid foundation and have oriented ourselves to consider the next short but significant question, the second course in eating the elephant—Where. This is our Vision Statement, which describes the organization in a future successful state, 7 to 10 years in the future. What will the business look like when it achieves what we set out to achieve?

With a Vision Statement, as with most documents, there's an inverse relationship between complexity and clarity. The more complex a Vision Statement is, the less likely that it provides clear and simple guidance. Complex Vision Statements only worsen Blurred Vision. If we cannot describe the vision of our company, in detail, in less than five minutes, we are suffering from Blurred Vision.

Burt Nanus, Professor Emeritus at the University of Southern California's Marshall School of Business, makes some great points about the value of a company's vision. He says it clarifies the purpose and direction of the company. It inspires enthusiasm and encourages commitment. Perhaps most importantly, Vision Statements "prevent people from being overwhelmed by immediate problems because they help distinguish what is truly important from what is merely interesting."

With our Vision Statement on paper, it's a good time to take a little reality check, one that will save us a lot of anguish, disappointment, and ... possibly ... the stalling of our business. In answering our Why, we did some introspection about what we want out of life. Now that we've also developed our Vision Statement, we need to ask ourself if the business we're in is the best vehicle to achieve our vision. If it's not, then it's unlikely we will continue to find managing our business to be energizing and rewarding.

Once we know Why we're in business and Where we want to go, it's time for the third course in eating the elephant—clarifying the vision of our business by exploring the How.

The How is our plan, our business plan as well as our life plan. Exactly how do we plan to reach the vision we've set for the company? What are the things we're going to do this year to move us closer to realizing our vision for ourself and the company? What are we going to do this quarter? This month? Today?

Just as with our Why and Where, we need to write down the How if we expect to share and accomplish it. Simply thinking about increasing sales, securing an expansion loan, or finding someone to help manage our business is unlikely to make them happen. If we expect to get results in our business, we need to plan our work and then work our plan ... a plan that's written down and available for others to see, discuss, and implement.

Our head may be spinning with all the deep thinking and visioning we've been doing, but that's only the starting point. Following through on the plan is where the real work takes place and where the results are delivered. But that work will be greatly accelerated because now the workers are working together, working from a plan, and working toward the same goals.

Sharing is Caring

Congratulations! We've taken all those thoughts about our business that formerly lived only as electrical impulses between the neurons in our brain and captured them in a document. Now it's time to start sharing it with others and clue them in as to what our business is all about and where it's headed. Who is the "them" we should share it with? This includes all our employees, of course. They will find comfort and security in knowing the company they work for has a vision beyond the next year and that it will continue to provide them with employment into the future.

Naturally, we might not want to share all the details of the plan with everyone in the company. So, we need to be selective. But we also need to share enough of the plan to give our people a clear picture of where the company is headed, why their work is important, and how their work fits into it.

It may also be appropriate to share some of our thinking with customers and suppliers. A well-crafted vision will be enlightening to everyone who touches or is touched by our business.

Hopefully, we achieved the simplicity that's essential to a well-crafted vision. We don't want people to scratch their heads and try to figure out what it means. Instead, we want them to read or hear it and know immediately what they need to do to make it happen. Or perhaps we will be surprised to discover that they read it but aren't sure they see the wisdom of our carefully considered vision for the company. This can be tough for entrepreneurs.

We really never had to justify any of our actions as a young business owner. For one thing, there was no one to justify them to because it was just us. For another, it was our business and we could run it anyway we darn well pleased. But then our baby business started to mature. Just as teenagers challenging their parents is a healthy and normal part of growing up, it is healthy and normal for our employees to challenge us regarding our vision for the business. What's absolutely essential is to not see these challenges as an uprising but as a great opportunity to hone that vision.

We must assume positive intent on the part of our employees, not take the position that they think we are dumb or foolish. Instead, take the position that these are smart people who quite possibly, and most probably, are better informed about some aspects of our operation or the market than we are. Their knowledge should be one of the reasons we hired them to join the company. Now's the time to respect that knowledge and see their challenges for what they are: well-intentioned efforts to ensure that our vision is sound.

Just as a ship sails fastest against the wind,[6] these challenges from employees can be a force that accelerates the progress and profitability of our business.

Speaking of ships reminds me of a friend who took a four-day sailing adventure off the coast of Maine in a two-masted schooner built in 1871.[7] For years, guests had asked if they could climb the ratlines, the cargo-net style rigging used to go aloft and work the sails. The captain finally relented and purchased some harnesses and rigging to ensure the safety of passengers who wanted to see the seas from 50 feet above the water.

My friend was one of the first to have the opportunity to climb to the top of the mast. He donned his harness, clipped on the safety rope, and began to climb. His daughter, the ship's mate, held the safety line. After about five feet he paused, nodded to his daughter, and stepped sideways off the ratline, falling a few feet before the safety line arrested his fall. The captain was appalled, but my friend, who had rock-climbing experience, explained this was a standard practice. It tested the safety arrangement and assured the person holding the safety line that they could safely arrest the fall. Better to do that at five feet than 50.

The captain, a veteran sailor but know-nothing regarding climbing safety, prohibited further test falls.

When our bright, energized employees test our ideas, there may be a few instances when they do so to embarrass or spite us. It is far more likely, though, that they want to make sure the ideas are sound, well-considered, and the best option to accomplish the objective. Our employees understand that a rising tide raises all ships. What's good for the company is good for them. The fact that it's good for us is a nice bonus.

That's not to say we should blithely accept every comment, concern, and criticism. We should defend our thinking and measure it against theirs. Doing so will not only ensure that the vision is tried and tested, but it reinforces our image as an owner who values employee input. We ignore their input at our peril, because they will soon stop offering it, resulting in a team of robots blindly following our golden edicts and enlightened guidance.

Most of us can probably recall an incident in our past when a superior discarded our best advice on how to make an improvement or avoid some problem. We probably shook off that snub, but the next time a problem came up, we may have decided it would be a perfect payback to just let it happen and hope the fallout rained down on that arrogant SOB. It's probably not our proudest moment, but it's a very human response. We need to be sure not to create an environment where we could be the victim of that kind of retaliation.

It's far better to have employees who recognize us as a willing listener, someone genuinely interested in their input on how to do things better. If we build that kind of relationship with our employees, not only will they embrace our vision, but they will serve as our early warning system. They will be eager to let us know when something is going wrong or we're headed off course, and just as eager to do whatever they can to get us back on track.

Capturing our vision in a written form, sharing it with others, and vetting it against their questions and concerns moves us well down the path to correcting our blurred vision. The last thing to do to optimize our organization's optics is to live the vision. Articulate the words through our actions. Give our employees not just a document to refer to but a visual roadmap to follow. There's no more apt application of the old saying that actions speak louder than words. We need to make sure our employees not only hear our vision for the company, but that they see it in our actions.

Seeing a Successful Future

Regardless of how blurred our vision may be today, there's no magic to correcting it to 20/20, as one of my clients found.

> This client was facing the very real possibility of going out of business. This was an established, family-owned company that was well-known and well-respected in its community. The family's taxable earnings had once placed them in the top 1% of North American income earners, but when they contacted me they were staring down the barrel of a gun called insolvency.
>
> The focus that helped them to achieve earlier success had been diluted and diffused. Decades of hard work had unraveled over a short 18-month timeframe. The client had lost their way, and the future of the company was threatened.
>
> The owners committed to narrowing their focus to just three things:
> - increase profitable sales by aggressively pursuing proven markets
> - eliminate all unnecessary expenditures
> - speed up cash flow by shrinking invoicing time and by aggressively collecting outstanding receivables.
>
> Of course, they didn't forego the other basic business functions, but those were handled by the capable members of the company's team. When it came to the critical business initiatives that the owners devoted the bulk of their attention to, their focus was primarily on the three priorities they had identified.

The good news is they recovered, but they came away chastened by the knowledge that having blurred vision is the norm and it can always return. Maintaining clear vision requires constant attention, and without that clear vision, they know they are likely to find themselves reliving the same frightening scenario.

....

A blurred vision can be easily corrected, but it may require that we take on yet another title: COO, Chief Optical Officer. We need to regularly evaluate our company's vision. Is it clear, focused, and shared with everyone in the organization? If not, then it's time for corrective action. We need to ask ourselves what must be done to sharpen our organizational vision and get it to 20/20.

CHAPTER 3
NO ACCOUNTABILITY

Symptoms

We have a love-hate relationship with cowboys but heavier on the love.

There is certainly a lot to love. Cowboys represent the things that most Americans find special pride in. They are hardy sorts with a hard way of life. While they tend to all manner of tasks around the ranch, the vision most people hold of the cowboy is a man out on the range. In the early days of The West, herds of cattle were left to graze on the as-yet-unfenced, open land. Every year, the cowboys would round them up for branding and to sort out the mature animals for market.

Before the mid-19th century, most of the cattle were raised to meet the needs of the rancher, with any surplus meat and hides sold locally. But after the end of the American Civil War, as large meat-packing plants began to open in Chicago and other cities, a new and profitable market for meat opened. That fostered the birth of the cattle drive, with cowboys moving large herds across the grazing areas to a railhead where the cattle could be loaded onto trains for their one-way trip to the meat-packing plant.

Whether at the ranch, on a round-up, or driving cattle to market, the cowboys endured all manner of weather, dawn-to-dusk work, uncooperative cattle, and the constant risk of injury or death. Their bravery and grit are traits still much admired today.

With those facts forming the basis of our cowboy lore, the publishing industry and Hollywood piled on a healthy layer of myth. On the big screen there was Audie Murphy, Gene Autry, and of course, John Wayne. Television introduced us to the Cartwrights (*Bonanza*), Chuck Connors (*The Rifleman*), and James Garner (*Maverick*).

Without exception, these fictional cowboys exemplified what we felt were the best traits of our country. They were honest and ever-reliable, men you could trust your life to without a second thought. They were strong and good looking but never boastful. They weren't afraid to fight and always fought fair, regardless of the under-handed, low-down, no-good tricks of the bad guys. And you could always count on them to show up in the nick of time.

They tended to be independent, a characteristic much admired by their fans. Guided by an internal code and strong ethics, cowboys did what they thought was right regardless of the consequences.

So much to love! So where does the hate come in? Largely from that independent streak. While being independent can be an admirable trait, it has some definite downsides. When people today use the adjective *cowboy* to describe someone else, it's usually in a derogatory sense. In this context, the term describes someone who does whatever they think is best with no regard for the consequences to anyone else. Some of the adjectives related to the negative connotations of being a cowboy include foolish, dangerous, reckless, and aggressive.

Cowboys, in the negative sense, are the anti-organization person, answerable to no one but themselves. The manager afflicted with the trait of No Accountability is a modern-day cowboy. While a lack of accountability may have been tolerable for the old-time cowboy whose leadership responsibilities consisted of chasing off coyotes, herding cattle, and having the occasional encounter with a bad guy. But not being accountable is a major drawback when it comes to leading a business in our modern world.

One of the main reasons we start our own business is to achieve some form of independence. This is a solid reason to set out on our own, but many entrepreneurs confuse the words *independent* with *unaccountable*. When there's no accountability in an organization, there usually follows a lack of discipline. When there's no discipline, the performance of the company suffers. When performance suffers long enough, the business fails.

Too often entrepreneurs view ourselves as freewheeling mavericks who expect allegiance from everyone but accountability to no one. Let's face it, many people become small business owners because we just didn't fit in the corporate world. We either couldn't, or simply wouldn't, get along in a corporate climate.

The unfortunate fact is that some of the very things we disliked most about corporate life—structure, accountability, and discipline—are the very things that we need most in our own business.

While we're on the topic of The West, let's talk about arrows. The modern cowboys of business are great at shooting them; lots of them. It's one of the symptoms of No Accountability. They don't set performance or financial targets and then hold themselves accountable for reaching them. Instead they shoot arrows, then put the targets where the arrows landed and call it success.

I've worked with companies where the owner didn't pay much attention to profit or other performance metrics during the year. Then at the end of the year, they'd look at their annual results and evaluate their success. Well, in their mind they were evaluating success but against what KPI, goal, or target?

Say the company did $1.4 million in a year. Was that a good year? There's absolutely no way to answer this question without knowing our goals or past performance. To determine if it was a good year, we need to ask some other questions, possibly inquiries such as, "What was the target?" or "Was that an improvement over last year?" or "What was spent to reach that level of sales?"

One of my early clients was a midsize, multimillion dollar construction company with tons of equipment. They would go all year and track nothing—not job cost, not financial risk, not quality. Nothing! They would go through the entire year not knowing if they made any money.

The only reason they ever knew how well or how poorly the company did was because they had to file their annual taxes.[8] If, in the owner's estimation, the company had done well, then it was high fives all around and bonus checks as a reward. If the company hadn't performed at whatever level the owner had in mind, then they shook their heads, muttered a "shucks" or two, and expressed the hope that they would do better next year ... and bonus checks were still handed out! This company was a model of No Accountability. As a construction company, the one thing they were good at was digging a hole they couldn't get out of.

Out of sight ... out of control.

I hadn't intended to ride this cowboy theme quite so long, but there is one more symptom of No Accountability with a cowpoke connection. How many cowboy movies include a saloon scene with a high-stakes poker game? The room is usually crowded and smoky, frowzy barmaids circulate the room, as the barkeep (with the mandatory apron) slides shots of whiskey down the bar to eager patrons. In poker, the best bluffer is often the big winner, but winning with that strategy requires displaying confidence even when you're holding five cards that don't come together in any possible winning combination. And, of course, if anyone gets a peek at those cards—maybe like one of the barmaids who just might be an accomplice of the opponent across the table—the jig is up. So, players ensure that no one catches on to their bluff by keeping their cards close to their chest, shielding them from prying eyes.

As a business owner afflicted with No Accountability, we do the same with our cards ... which in this case are our plans and goals for the business. It's not that we are worried about having someone steal a glance and tip off one of the other players in our market about a restoration innovation, technical breakthrough, or remarkable marketing scheme. Quite the opposite. We don't want anyone to see our hand because it's so lousy. This is similar to how we hold our cards close to our chest when our vision is blurred.

Secrecy is our friend. The less others know about how the business is performing, the better. That way no one can call our management or decision making into question. If the numbers look lousy and the banker sees them, we worry about the availability of future loans or the possibility of our debt being called in. If our spouse gets an eyeful of how things are going, it might rekindle those conversations about getting a real job. And if our employees get a look at our hand, they might wonder if now wouldn't be a good time to start polishing up their résumé and searching the internet for a new employer.

Owners who hold their cards close keep business performance data out of sight; exactly where they want it. This means less pressure on the owner, but it also means the business is largely out of control. With no defined targets and, therefore, no possibility of any accountability, the business stumbles along aimlessly. You can't really say it's off course; it simply has no course.

Good employees are likely to detect this lack of control eventually and, out of concern for their livelihood, begin to press the business owner about the company's direction and progress. Business owners who lack accountability know this, so many choose not to hire employees who are likely to ask such questions.

Instead, they hire weak employees. No Accountability managers are more comfortable with employees who either lack the business acumen to detect that the company has no direction, or who lack the courage to raise the issue with the owner. These managers want employees who are simply happy to have a job. Surrounding themselves with these types of employees reduces the number of those who might actually attempt to hold the business owner accountable. However, these aren't the employees who are likely to drive the business to higher levels of success.

Independent Isn't Unaccountable

Some business owners confuse independence with unaccountability. Independence is freedom from outside control, something that many entrepreneurs greatly cherish. For many business owners, having the levers of success firmly in our own hands was one of the main reasons we broke away from simple employment and chose the entrepreneurial path instead.

As an independent businessperson, we are relatively free to manage our business in the way we think best. Independence is one of the foundations of free enterprise.

Of course, that kind of complete independence is an illusion. Any businessperson can list the alphabet soup of outside agencies and authorities we have to deal with on a daily basis. At the federal level there's the IRS, OSHA, EPA, and the FLRA, plus the state and local regulators. They impose innumerable limitations on what we can and cannot do. While America remains one of the great global bastions of free enterprise, it comes with many restrictions. With those restrictions come regulatory accountability.

And then there are the people who surround our business. They include family, customers, employees, and suppliers. Good owners feel an accountability to these people, hopefully in the order shown. Without them, business success will be about as hard to find as the Tooth Fairy[9] riding in Santa's sleigh helping the Easter Bunny deliver eggs.

And last but far from least are the family members who depend on us and our business to keep a roof over their heads. We are, compared to entrepreneurs around the globe, among the most independent business owners on the planet. Still, we are highly accountable to a good many people.

We are almost certainly more accountable now than when we started our business. Back when the business was new and we were likely the only person engaged in routine operations, being unaccountable had a valuable, liberating effect on our management approach. We had near-total freedom to make changes to the business as we saw fit. We could instantly tweak things when we identified a new or better way. Or, when we just didn't feel like doing those things. We could immediately adjust when an unpredicted roadblock appeared. We were agile, nimble, and flexible—all very good things for an upstart business.

But there was still accountability. Probably the heaviest accountability was what we placed on ourself. We were the one who had to get up early to take care of things in the office before customers started calling. When the workday ended for most people, we had to go back to the office (probably our kitchen table) to process the day's paperwork and prep for the next day. There was no one pushing us to do these things. We did what we knew had to be done to make the business go and grow. Independent? Yes! Accountable? Absolutely. We were accountable to the person who has probably always been our toughest taskmaster and overseer—ourself.

Punctuality is a popular performance standard that many of us have addressed at one time or another. "If you show up late one more time, don't even bother to come in!" we shout at the once-again-tardy employee. And in the heat of the moment, we mean it. But faced with having to cover the workload for the employee if we actually follow through on our threat, we're tempted to let it slide when they show up late again (maybe there really was a traffic jam) and turn a blind eye to the tardiness one more time.

Throwing family relationships into the business mix, our tolerance for bending performance standards in the company can make us question the value of setting standards in the first place. When we consider that as many as 90% of all business enterprises in North America are considered "family" businesses, this makes for a lot of standard bending! We weigh the benefit of drawing a line in the sand when it comes to holding a performance standard against the odds of having an unpleasant holiday dinner if we do.

Causes

The Land of Milk and Honey

I described how owners suffering from No Accountability is a common trait in startup businesses, but a lack of accountability can also make a sudden appearance at a later and surprising point in the life of a business. If we have a lifestyle business, we will, hopefully, reach the point where we can lean back in our chair and say with well-deserved pride, "I did it!" We built our business to the size we envisioned, we have things running smoothly, and we could be perfectly content to cruise along like this for years to come.

We deserve to cruise for a while! We've put in the long hours and shed buckets of blood, sweat, and tears. Why shouldn't we be able to kick back, take it easy, and let other people worry about the business? Isn't it time to let others shoulder the load while we just go along for the ride?

A good sign we've reached this point is a sudden, intense interest in big, expensive toys. Time to build that swimming pool, buy that boat, or invest in that second home. We feel we deserve to reap the rewards of getting our business to its current, solid status.

We do deserve those kinds of things. I'm not ashamed to say I've acquired a few of those for myself. My wife and I live in a beautiful lakeside home, and on nice days I drive to work in a too-fast-and-too-small-to-be-practical sports car. But while the success of my business enabled me to acquire a few nice things along the way, that doesn't mean that I got complacent about my business. I hold myself just as accountable now as I ever did. In fact, the accountability may have increased because I now have a larger team that depends on the business remaining successful.

My reputation as a consultant is based, in part, on the success of my company, Violand Management Associates. And while the company is certainly not perfect, it's hard to hold myself out to others as an example of how to be a successful entrepreneur unless I have a successful business to point to as an example. I am accountable to my clients and readers to demonstrate effective management techniques.

I understand how, after years of labor and toil to build a business and of being held accountable to others, we want to be free from that weight. We've been living for other people all those years; how about a little me time and let someone else take on the responsibility and the accountability?

Success does not give us a free pass regarding accountability. In most cases, the exact opposite is true. As the business expands, so do our accountabilities. Unless we're ready to cash out of the business, we need to stop patting ourself on the back and continue to fulfill our responsibilities to the people who rely on us.

Fear of Success

We explored how one of the symptoms of No Accountability is that the owner keeps their cards close to the chest because they fear showing their weak hand. Oddly, there's another fear that is one of the primary causes of No Accountability. It's the fear of success.

Most entrepreneurs are comfortable with the fear of failure. We know what failure looks like. We know about the financial and personal consequences. These fears are relatively quantifiable, so we are able to do a mental risk analysis and determine whether or not the potential benefits outweigh those risks. We may even feel somewhat invigorated by the prospect of failure.

Winston Churchill said, "Nothing in life is so exhilarating as to be shot at without result." Facing great risks is exhilarating. If there were no risks, there would be no challenges to meet and no sense of accomplishment if and when those challenges were overcome. Entrepreneurs take pride in exhibiting the courage and bravery required to launch a business, and we often sneer at those who lack the nerve to do likewise and choose to remain just another cog in some big company.

While entrepreneurs can deal with the known fears of failure, success represents more of an unknown. We have some gauzy notion of being financially comfortable and respected as that greatest paragon of free enterprise, the successful small businessperson. But what we are unable to see clearly, the thing that frightens us more than failure to launch our business, is not knowing whether we can actually manage a successful company.

I read the statement somewhere that most Americans are better at attaining than they are at maintaining. We love obstacles to overcome, mountains to climb, and rivers to ford. Getting a small business off the ground is nothing to sneeze at, but with a good idea backed by some cash and grit, many people are able to launch one. Maintaining it is something else. That requires a much better-stocked toolbox of skills; skills we may fear we lack.

There are five essential functions of management: planning, organizing, staffing, leading, and controlling. That's a lot of things that an entrepreneur must do well to manage their business. As the organization grows, decisions need to be made about equipment purchases, hiring and firing, accounting methods, key performance indicators, and a hundred other things to sustain the business that require knowledge far beyond what was required of our one-man operation.

Swollen Ego

The sixth and final conspirator described in this book is Swollen Ego. While this trait creates its own, unique set of obstacles to our success, it also conspires to encourage No Accountability.

Managers who suffer from Swollen Ego will feed ourselves on a steady diet of positive self-talk about our extraordinary business skills. We believe we are naturally endowed with a superior set of skills that will carry us to the Nirvana of organizational success powered almost exclusively by our personal talents and knowledge.

Since we believe ourself to be superior to others in such matters, why would we feel the need to be held accountable for our actions? Why should we be held accountable to others when we fundamentally feel that we know how to run our business better than anyone else?

Most entrepreneurs do possess a special drive and determination that others don't share. But when it comes to business skills, we are often no better ... and in too many cases, worse ... than others. A great check on our ability to successfully manage the business is to identify goals and objectives, and then hold ourself accountable for achieving them.

Consequences

Management by Swarm
Years ago, as I was coaching one of my kid's soccer practices, I noticed a group of five- or six-year-olds practicing on the adjoining field. They were falling into a familiar pattern that so many young children do as they learn the sport; it's what some refer to as "swarm soccer" and what I observed was a classic example. Every one of the kids was chasing the ball; nobody was holding back. The only players who were standing outside the swarm to receive the ball—should one of the kids tangled in the swarm get lucky enough to actually kick it beyond the forest of shins—were the goalies. These two kids were standing in front of their respective goals, bored out of their minds, and passing the time picking clover.

Eventually, the kids learn that their roles on the field shift as the ball moves from person to person. They come to realize that they sometimes need to carry the ball, sometimes position themselves to receive the ball, sometimes try to take the ball from the other team, and sometimes defend their goal from an attack by their opponents. But until they understand their responsibilities in the shifting flow of the game, their intense focus is on furiously kicking at the ball with their little legs until one of them eventually lands a solid kick that sends the ball down the field with the swarm in hot pursuit.

In a No Accountability organization, the efforts of our employees will resemble those of these budding Beckhams.[10] Absent clear goals that form the underpinning of accountability, they have no understanding of their responsibilities in the organization. They aren't sure what they should be focused on, so they devote their attention to whatever issue is at hand at the time.

I'm not the only one who has recognized this similarity between young soccer players and employees of organizations where the owner lacks accountability. Dr. Ichak Adizes noticed it, too, and wrote about it in his book, *The Pursuit of Prime.* He observed, "People do not know who is accountable for what. The organization acts like a team of small children playing soccer: every one of them goes for the ball, and, from the sidelines, they look like a swarm of locusts moving around the field. They all try to kick the ball and end up kicking one another in the shins and crying. Their coaches spend time lecturing the children on the value of teamwork. 'Stop fighting,' they tell the kids, 'and help each other.'

The coaches' speeches fall on deaf ears because the kids have no idea how to play as a team. The coaches have to tell them what their positions are and that they must stick to those positions in a way that does not ignore the ball."

Swarm management doesn't just exist in new or in smaller companies, either. I've seen it in multimillion-dollar companies, and I've seen it in companies that have been around for generations. When swarm management is displayed in a pee-wee soccer league, it can be adorable—except to the coaches. But, when it's displayed in a business, it's tragic.

Weakening The Roster

Putting yourself in the jersey of a young soccer player, you can imagine why many kids fail to see the fun in the sport. Mashing together in a scrum and getting flailed on the shins doesn't hold much attraction for the average kid. What they feel is frustration and disappointment at not accomplishing something.

So, too, for our employees. Most people seek and enjoy the positive feedback and sense of accomplishment that comes from meeting their objectives and fulfilling their responsibilities. Those are feelings that are hard to come by in an organization owned or operated by a No Accountability leader. With no clear goals, it's impossible for employees to know when they've done the job their boss expects.

This makes it difficult to provide actionable performance feedback. What is possible are statements of praise like, "Thanks for the great job you did on that project" for good performance or "You really need to work a bit harder" when they fall short of our perceived (but unknown to everyone else) standards. When employees are held accountable for specific metrics and activities, that provides the basis for feedback that will actually drive performance improvement and create personal satisfaction.

"Kelly, congratulations on hitting the target of a 10% increase in the number of calls you made to contractors last week." Now Kelly knows what she did right and what she should strive to do more of.

"Kelly, you got the numbers to me by today's deadline, but they were missing the figures I requested about the average daily amount of each chemical we use." Again,

Kelly was given a specific accountability. In this case she failed to achieve it, but knowing what she was accountable for gave her a specific goal to work toward and precise metrics that can be used to gauge her performance.

It also avoids the scenario of seemingly random rewards. Say an employee somehow achieves something that, coincidentally, was on the owner's radar that day. As a result, that employee earned some recognition from the boss. While the employee, no doubt, appreciates kudos, it won't be very effective in encouraging future performance. Others on the team will be similarly mystified about what it was the employee did that earned them an attaboy.

We can certainly find employees who will thrive in this kind of environment. They take a "whatever" attitude about their jobs. No accountability at the top for leadership or management? Whatever. That makes life simple for these employees, because they know they won't or can't be held accountable, either. There's no motivation for them to jump higher, because they don't know where the bar is. There's no reason for them to go faster, because they have no idea what direction they should take. There's no sense in going the extra mile, because there's a good chance they will end up a mile from where the boss wants them to be.

We can find plenty of these "whatever" employees available in the market, because good managers get them out of their organizations as quickly as possible. No Accountability managers, on the other hand, are happy to have them on their team because the "whatevers" don't exert any pressure on the manager to perform or expect other employees to perform.

The "A" players, on the other hand, find this type of management intolerable. They thrive on meeting goals and pursuing higher levels of performance. Star performers want—they need—a chance to shine. Without that chance, they will take their skills and talents elsewhere.

Time for An Accounting
The toll that having a manager without accountability takes on an organization isn't fast or probably noticeable. Instead, it is a long-term erosion. The brain drain that occurs as our most talented team members seek other opportunities saps the talent, energy, and capability of the company. It becomes just another vanilla organization with no chance for market distinction or higher performance. And over time, the owner and their accountant will see the toll it takes in the declining bottom line.

With the problems described previously, it's obvious that growth will stall. Some of that will be because we lack the fuel for growth; an engaged and interested team. Having no accountability depletes employee enthusiasm. They may very well give their best (although it's unlikely), but because their efforts are unguided, their efforts may be wasted. It doesn't take much of this to leave our employees disinterested and disengaged.

Along with destroying our employees' enthusiasm, or as a result of it, we soon discover there isn't enough money to grow the business. This means we need to go knocking on the doors of banks, trying to convince them to front us the funds to renew our business. But when No Accountability is the cause of poor performance, we've put ourselves in a real bind. What got us in our predicament was a lack of accountability, and accountability is exactly what the banks will insist on before we'll see a nickel.

Of course, as with each of the six behaviors that conspire to destroy our business, there are ways to steer clear of the painful outcomes of No Accountability.

Solutions

Reevaluate Your Debts

We already talked about how the Inflated Ego trait tends to create unaccountable managers. A good place to start building some accountability is for us to simply get over ourselves. As hard as it may be for some business owners to accept, we need to realize that the planets do not revolve around us. Although, as a small business owner, we DO play a pivotal role in the economy of our community and, in fact, our country.

When any politician starts making a speech, we don't have to wait very long to hear them credit the critical importance of small businesses to our nation.[11] Every citizen owes a bit of gratitude to the people like us who are willing to take the risks involved in launching and running a business. But the first and biggest step we need to take to rid ourselves of the troubles caused by a lack of accountability is to realize not what we are owed but what we owe.

Former president Barack Obama was relentlessly criticized by his detractors for this statement he made in a campaign speech on July 13, 2012: "If you've been successful, you didn't get there on your own." That sounds like a slap in the face to everyone who has launched a business. But read in the context of his speech, we realize that his point was an accurate assessment that none of us succeeds alone.

Rather, business owners rely on and benefit from the input and contributions of others to support our success.

He captures the essence of his speech by saying, "The point is, is that when we succeed, we succeed because of our individual initiative, but also because we do things together."

The important takeaway from this speech, the one that's relevant to our topic of accountability, is contained in that last comment. In other words, we are mutually accountable to others.

Perhaps we do possess some skills that set us apart from most other business owners. In fact, that's highly likely. Knowing that fact nurtures the ego and encourages self-talk about amazing business skills. Still, we need others to help us capitalize on whatever special gifts and talents we have. We need others to leverage what we bring to the company and help put it into action. We need to realize that we owe something to others who helped (and continue to help) us succeed and that we are accountable to them.

So, who do we need to be accountable to? They are listed below, in what I believe is the order of importance.

Accountable to Family

Let's start with our family. Considering the fact that lots of people in business rely on family members as employees, there are actually two facets to this accountability: family who are strictly family, and family who are also employees. Let's look first at family members who are outside of the business.

Our accountability to family members is to live up to the often said but almost as often ignored aphorism that "family is first." I think we all believe it, and most of us think we live it, but we sometimes don't realize how poorly we practice it. A small business can be like a hungry beast that consumes a tremendous amount of our time, attention, and energy. We feed the beast all day, but sometimes it follows us home at night and on weekends like a hungry, stray dog looking for more.

And our inclination is to give it more. We do it grudgingly, typically justifying it in our heads that we're creating more income or building a better business that will, in the long run, guarantee a better life for our family. No doubt that's true, but in most cases family members would prefer to have more of us and less of the things that extra income will bring.

Dale Carnegie promoted a concept he called "day-tight compartments." The fundamental point of the concept was to not worry about the past or the future but to live in the moment. A perfect application of the concept is the need to close the door on work when we walk out the door. Leave work at work, so that when we are away from work, we are truly away from work and can be with our family.

That has never been more difficult than it is today. Back in 1936, when Carnegie wrote *How to Win Friends and Influence People*,[12] people who brought their work home had to physically tote it home, probably in a leather briefcase. Today we are able to work from home almost as easily as we do at our place of business. We use the computer in our home office to connect to our work, and it's almost like being there. Add our always-on communications via email and cell phone, and the line between work and home becomes so fuzzy as to almost disappear.

We need to draw the line and be with our family when the workday is done. They have made a tremendous investment in us. They support us, they believe in us, and they are our top cheerleaders. They understand that our work is what enables them to live a comfortable life. But the payoff for their investment in us should also be emotional. That payoff is far more valuable than newer cars, a bigger television, and a fancier house.

No doubt we've all heard the well-known quote that states, "No one on his death-bed ever said, 'I wish I had spent more time on my business.'" Believe it.

Accountable to Employees

We make a bargain with the people we hire to work for our business; they commit to doing what's expected of them, and we commit to paying them for meeting those expectations. As part of the bargain, we have mutual accountability to deliver on those commitments.

For their part, we can—and should—assess how well they live up to their end of the bargain through regular performance reviews. But how do they assess how well we fulfill our commitment? We could simply be satisfied with the fact that we give them a regular paycheck for the amount we agreed to pay them. That, however, is a pretty low standard. Good employees, the ones who will contribute the most to our success, will hold us accountable for more.

They will rightfully expect us to provide them with the tools and training necessary to perform their job to the best of their abilities. They will expect to be recognized for superior performance. They will expect reasonable opportunities for advancement based on that superior performance. Do they expect too much? Not if we want them to be dedicated, productive employees.

And then there's the issue of loyalty. There is precious little of that these days, going both ways. Many, perhaps most, employers, look first at cutting staff when things get tight and money has to be saved. And many, perhaps most, employees will eagerly jump ship if they perceive a better opportunity with another company.

But this situation makes it all the more unusual and valuable for companies to create an environment that makes employees want to stay put. Having loyal, long-time employees enables us to elevate the level of service we provide and reduces the hassle of constantly backfilling positions because of high turnover.

No leader will lead for long if they don't share a mutual respect for the people they lead. It's from them that we receive the authority to lead in the first place. And it is to them that we must hold ourselves accountable.

Accountable to Customers

The baseline here is that we are accountable to deliver the promised service to our customers, to do so professionally, and to an acceptable level of quality. Fail to meet this minimum standard and we will seldom be invited back to do the job again in the future.

To earn the loyalty of our customers, to have them spreading the gospel of our service excellence to friends and family, we need to hold ourselves accountable to something higher than that baseline service level. We should, instead, continually raise the bar on quality and service. Constantly look for ways to help make our customers' lives easier or help them do their jobs better, whether it's running a household, managing a company, or giving back to a community.

Our customers owe us nothing. We have the privilege of serving them, and that makes us accountable to our customers.

Accountable to Stakeholders

This one is pretty straightforward. If people provided us with money to build our business, we are accountable for paying it back. They will be particularly pleased if the amount returned is greater than the amount they invested.

This accountability, at its core, comes down to handing over a check to repay that debt at the promised time. Sometimes that's done as a lump sum, but more often our investors are involved over a longer time and repaid in installments. This raises some issues about what's reasonable for our investors to expect from us. Do they have any sort of input to operations or strategy, or are they silent partners who leave us to run the business in the way we think best?

Do they expect us to give them a look at the books so they can monitor how their investment is being put to work? If so, that makes us accountable for reporting our financials to them. This can be a big bone of contention with an entrepreneur. We aren't keen on people looking over our shoulder and asking us to justify why we bought this and why we spent that. It's reasonable for investors to hold us accountable for using the money appropriately, but how much insight into our operations and how much oversight we're willing to cede are things we should clearly agree upon before we take their money.

Investors often include family, and these investments are often done based on nothing more than trust between family members. They believe in us and our idea and are willing to support us with an infusion of their cash. Sometimes they do that strictly to help a member of the family and expect nothing more than the return of their investment. More often, and more appropriately, they expect some return on their investment.

Whatever their expectation, the details should be discussed, agreed to, and preferably documented. Write it down and sign it. Then talk about whether the investment gives them any right to expect that they have any say in our operation. Decide how and when repayment will occur. We may think these are details that can be worked out later, but more often than not, doing so results in disagreements and disputes.

Money can be a potent wedge in family relationships. Siblings that co-existed perfectly their entire lives often find themselves in bitter conflict when it comes to divvying up the estate of their departed parents. We must be sure not to allow a generous act by a family member, their willingness to help bankroll our dream, turn into a conflict that will sour the relationship.

Failing to hold ourselves accountable to a financial institution that invests in us may result in a ruined credit record. Failing to hold ourselves accountable to family members who invest in us can result in ruined relationships with the people closest to us.

Accountable to the Financial Community

I just mentioned financial institutions. Our accountability to them is typically clearly laid out and well documented. All those documents we signed when we took out our loan included the dozens of whereases and wherebys to which we shall be bound until such time as we shall repay them their due.

It goes without saying, but I will say it anyway, that we must live up to the commitments we make to the financial institutions we borrow from and do business with. Fines, penalties, and possible jail await us otherwise. But as everyone knows, from the lowliest platform personnel[13] to the CEO of every bank, from the smallest community S&L to the too-big-to-fail giants, there's some wiggle room in many financial transactions. Avoid wiggling.

Whether dealing with financial institutions, suppliers, customers, or others, we must hold ourselves accountable to the highest standards of personal and financial integrity. Leave those corners uncut. Avoid the slippery deals. Pass up the too-good-to-be-true deals. They all offer short-term gain and may seem to present a low threat of any repercussions. The truth is, in almost every case, we will successfully skate by and suffer no adverse results from our semi-ill-gotten gains. The chances of getting caught are slim.

We should hold ourselves accountable to a higher standard. Again, the chances of getting caught are always small, but if we get caught doing something above and beyond the expected standards of ethical behavior, we've just leveled up to a higher stature in the eyes of the person who found us out. How much better is that than being caught in some under-the-table chicanery?

When it comes to our financial reporting, they have a right to hold us accountable, and we will be the better for it.

That's a lot of people to hold ourselves accountable to. But the fact is, if we're going to lead our organization into the future, then we're accountable to everyone we touch in our business.

Hold Others Accountable

I mentioned holding employees accountable. Doing so requires having a well-defined organization that specifies the roles of all the players. When our company is small, our organizational chart is straightforward and easy to understand. Everybody reports to the owner. If orders are given, it's usually the owner who does the giving. Either by accident or by design, we start our business with a structure that works well. Everybody knows what their job is and does it reasonably well. Things seem to click along smoothly.

Then things change: sales grow, employees are added, and the balance that seemed to work so well in our smaller company—where everyone knew what their responsibilities were and where all the bases were covered—doesn't work anymore. As our company grows, it's easy for our organization to mutate into a confusing mess where people don't know what they're responsibilities are, employees are afraid to make even minor decisions, and two or three people are doing what only one should be doing. Frequently, these companies' chains of command look more like what author Dr. Leon Danco calls obedience charts than they do organization charts, as everybody continues to report to the owner.

Sometimes people get added to the company so quickly that nobody takes the time to reassign job responsibilities. Or perhaps old, loyal employees have worn a rut in their jobs and don't want (or simply aren't qualified) to do jobs that need to be done in our larger company. So, we add even more people to the payroll in a Band-Aid attempt to plug the holes and stop the bleeding. We might add someone to help with invoicing, or chase receivables, or answer the phone, or return our phone calls. Maybe it's somebody to supervise projects, estimate work, and keep the warehouse organized. Or maybe all of the above! Before long the structure of the company has morphed into a creature that nobody recognizes and is neither efficient nor a fun place to work.

Too often we feel we don't have the time, or we don't have the patience, to organize our people and our company correctly as it grows. Instead, we waste countless hours and precious emotional energy breaking up petty squabbles or soothing the bruised egos of employees involved in internal turf wars. We race around redoing jobs and fixing customer relationships as jobs fall through the cracks because nobody knows who is responsible for what ... or at least that's what they say.

Many small business owners have never had the experience of working for a well-organized, large company. Others have had the misfortune of working for poorly organized, dysfunctional, small companies. As a result, we don't know how to structure our own company as it grows. This lack of understanding is a very common reason so many small businesses don't have the structure to grow into larger businesses. The organizational structure must expand and adjust as our company grows, just like our skeleton grows and adjusts as our body grows. Both are designed to support the structures for which they serve as the framework.

Adding to the problem is that fact that most entrepreneurs are caring and generous people. So, it's only natural that we would use our greatest physical asset—our business—to help our family and friends by providing employment for them. As a result, when a family member or a friend approaches us about a job, or when we feel these people can do better at our company, we hire them.

We hire high school buddies, college buddies, friends from the gym, people we meet at church, people we meet at the bar, neighbors, friends of neighbors. The list seems endless. Now, let's really shake things up by adding wives, husbands, girlfriends, boyfriends, sons, daughters, brothers, sisters, mothers, fathers, cousins, nephews, nieces, uncles, aunts, and any members of the gene pool I might have overlooked. These are people we love, people we want to share in our successful venture, but who may not be qualified for the jobs we have available.

So we build jobs and our organization around the skills people have or lack. This results in something akin to the experience of the man who went to the low-price tailor for a custom suit. When the man tries on the suit, he notices one sleeve is too long. The tailor tells him to pull one hand in a bit and bend his arm.

The customer comments that one of the shoulders droops a bit. The tailor suggests that he lift that shoulder slightly. The man observes that the back of the coat is too wide. The tailor tells him to bend forward slightly.

Having made all the physical adjustments, the customer hobbles out of the shop in a contorted posture: arm half-bent, one shoulder higher than the other, hunch-backed. Two women passing by see him leaving the tailor's shop, and one whispers to the other, "Look at that poor, crippled man."

"But," her friend answers, "look how beautifully the suit fits him."

We can't hold employees accountable unless they know what they are supposed to do and who they are supposed to do it for. This requires an organization chart. But the chart needs to be grounded in the needs of the business, not in the needs and limitations of the employees.

Recalibrate for the Successful Business
In their book, *Extreme Ownership: How U.S. Navy SEALs Lead and Win*, authors Jocko Willink and Leif Babin build the case for leaders taking 100% ownership of the decisions they make and the results produced by the organizations they lead. This principle applies to all levels of leadership throughout an organization, whether it's owning the business, managing a division, or running a project. It also applies to all areas of a business, whether it's sales results, jobs being completed on time, or even morale within the company. If we're in charge of producing results, we are accountable for the outcomes, both good and bad.

It might be helpful to mention that Willink and Babin are themselves ex-Navy SEALs, that they fought in the battle of Ramadi, Iraq, and that the decisions they made on the job frequently determined whether the people they led would make it home safely or at all. While the decisions most of us make in business will never lead to such life-or-death consequences, the principle of 100% ownership and accountability still applies.

One of the points made in the book really got my attention. A story was told about a conversation with the Chief Technology Officer of a large corporation whose division was falling behind. The CTO was doing his best to deflect responsibility for the shortfall by making excuses and blaming others. The authors called him out by stating, "When it comes to performance standards, it's not what you preach, it's what you tolerate." It's what we tolerate; how true is that?! And who among us hasn't been guilty, at least occasionally, of tolerating performance well short of a standard we had earlier mandated?

Discipline is one of the characteristics that separates great leaders from the rest. Tolerating subpar performance or not taking 100% ownership of our actions are deeper expressions of a lack of personal discipline. When it comes to whether our company is performing or falling short, it all returns to the same thing: it's not what we preach, it's what we tolerate. It's holding ourselves, and everyone we touch in the course of operating our business, accountable.

CHAPTER 4
HEROIC MANAGING

We love heroes. This fact worked out very well for Stan Lee. He was formerly editor-in-chief of Marvel Comics where, with several co-creators, he cranked out comic books featuring superheroes like Spider Man, the Hulk, the Fantastic Four, Iron Man, Daredevil, Thor, and many others beginning in the early 1960s.

Most boys my age grew up reading and trading those comics. Today, we have grown to adults who, as parents, gleefully take our kids to see the same heroes on the big screen at the movie theaters. Now, of course, the superheros are 30 feet tall and in 3D and HD sound instead of words and pictures on the pages of comic books. I am sure Lee was already quite well off, but I can only imagine the money that rolled in from all the royalties the movies, shirts, games, and other superhero-related merchandise generated in recent years.[14]

We also have our real-life heroes. We can probably think of someone from our youth who played a big part in our life; someone who was a personal hero. Various organizations celebrate people for their over-and-above efforts. For example, 2017's 10 CNN heroes included Stan Hays, a grand champion pitmaster who, through his nonprofit organization, prepared almost 1.7 million meals for disaster survivors and first responders.

And then there are business heroes, the people whose success we hope to emulate. For some, their heroes include the super-successful entrepreneurs who built massive companies such as Bill Gates (Microsoft) or Jeff Bezos (Amazon). For others, their business heroes are the visionaries such as Elon Musk who have been the driving force behind new technologies and industries. Yet others find their heroes in the businesspeople who succeed locally. They admire the men and women who create businesses that provide a comfortable living for their families and employees, and those who earn the respect of industry associations and their community members.

Search the internet for "qualities of a hero" and you will see many different traits listed by various publications and websites. A common thread, though, is that heroes are people who identify a problem or threat and solve it. For the different types of heroes named above, that works out well. All those heroes stepped up to help solve significant problems. Superheroes save us from alien invasions and all manner of villains. Business heroes build great companies, provide jobs, and contribute to the economy. Local heroes provide inspiration while making their communities better places for all who live in them.

But in some cases, the quest to solve problems creates new ones. Such is the plight of the Heroic Manager. Faced with a constant stream of issues and problems, we feel the need to personally resolve them. As the leader of our organization, it's easy to fall into the trap of being the chief problem solver. Don't get me wrong. Being able to solve problems is a critical part of being an effective leader, and making the big decisions is our job. But Heroic Managers don't stop at those big decisions. We eagerly take on the problems of everyone in the organization rather than allowing employees to make decisions for themselves.

As a Heroic Manager, for various reasons we will discuss, we feel the need to be the decider-in-chief, to the great detriment of our company.

Symptoms

Some organizational issues are difficult to detect. Not Heroic Managing. This is an issue that's relatively easy to spot.

When my company brings on a new client, we need to get to know their business very well before we begin offering advice. Some of our investigation is based on looking at the client's financials, organization chart, mission or vision, and other documents. But we also pretty quickly schedule a site visit. Walking around the company and talking to employees provides a separate and very valuable perspective about how the business is operated.

Our site visit includes interviews with key people. Our goal isn't to dig up dirt on the owner or to get people to tell us things that the owner is unlikely to admit. We do it to gauge the strength of the people and discover how they interact with one another and with the owner or managers.

If we discover that a company is staffed with relatively weak performers, that's usually a strong signal that there is Heroic Managing involved. Whether they subconsciously staff the organization with weak players who won't threaten their authority, or because they are simply not very good at hiring, Heroic Managers are typically surrounded by low performers.

When we find strong performers who indicate they are given little responsibility or authority, that's another telltale sign that Heroic Managing is making its presence felt. The manager with this condition is comfortable with being, and in fact is happy to be, the smartest person in the room and doesn't appreciate or need input from others.

The result is an underdeveloped, underperforming staff that is unlikely to take personal initiative. Any action or innovation must flow down from their manager. It is the "tyranny of the trivial," where the Heroic Manager holds a tight grip on every decision.

A friend told me about a meeting he attended as a mid-level manager at a global organization. An outside consultant was delivering her summary report to a group of about 15 people seated around a large conference table. The ranking member of the group was a vice president to whom many in the room reported.

It was a lengthy meeting that began in the morning and was scheduled to run to mid-afternoon. Late in the morning, the consultant said, "We can stop now and go to lunch a bit early, or I can keep going and be a few minutes late to break for lunch. What is your preference?" All the vice president's subordinates turned to him almost at once, as if their noses were tied to strings. It was clear that no one felt they should have an opinion; it was best to simply see what the VP wanted to do.

That incident stuck with my friend. It seemed evident that the people in the room knew very well that their opinion on whether to break or press on had no relevance. They had been trained to rely on their boss to tell them what he wanted. It left my friend believing that the VP probably expected the same deference from his subordinates in most decisions. While they would never be told to not speak up, they learned that doing so typically didn't bring positive outcomes for the employee who did. That type of situation puts a set of shackles on the energy and enthusiasm of employees.

We will typically find a command-and-control, military-style of leadership in companies owned or operated by Heroic Managers. "I say/you do" is the standard operating procedure.

People who work for Heroic Managers will tell us there is little delegation or distributed responsibility. The manager may be afraid that giving someone additional authority will result in the job being done very well, undermining their position as the most competent person in the organization. Or that the job won't be done as well as the manager could have done it theirself.

The range of potential assignments that the Heroic Manager believes requires their involvement vary from major operational decisions to things as simple as which paper to put in the copier. There is a right way to do everything, and the knowledge about the right way rests with the Heroic Manager.

Even when the manager does rely on an employee to handle some task or make a decision, they remain deeply involved and will micromanage the heck out of them.

Another indicator of the possible presence of Heroic Managing is an over-dependence on family members in the business. Considering that as many as 80% to 90%* of all business enterprises in North America are family controlled, that can be a very big challenge! Family members typically—but not always—can be counted on to do what the Heroic Manager would have done themselves. They are of one mind. And in many cases, they don't really need to be managed. We can rule them the way we have ruled our relationships with them our whole life.

A final symptom of Heroic Managing is that we take much of the credit for our company's accomplishments and achievements. That's fair, since we *are* making all the decisions. If things go well, then most of the credit rightfully belongs to us. But no one likes being on a team where one player gets all the credit. A mood of "why bother?" sets in, and employee creativity and problem-solving muscles atrophy.

Causes

Ask older folks where Clark Kent changed into his Superman outfit and they will probably tell you "in a phone booth." In both the comic books and some episodes of the TV show, he repeatedly used a phone booth as an impromptu changing room. In hindsight, that really didn't make a lot of sense considering the amount of privacy provided by a typical phone booth.[15]

For those of you old enough to have actually been in a phone booth, you know that getting out of a suit and into a full-body leotard would require some impressive contortions. The Man of Steel would be better off as the Man of Rubber to do the bending required. Of course, these are relatively small things we are asked to believe compared to the power to see through walls, fly, and deflect bullets with his bare hands.

So how does the average, mild-mannered business owner or manager transform into a Heroic Manager? In some cases, it comes about because of the seductiveness of being the chief problem solver. That's a role that's extremely difficult for most entrepreneurs and business managers to resist. For a Heroic Manager, the need to feel in control is almost tangible.

We relish the feeling of power as we tie on the cape and make the change from someone who values other people's opinions and is eager for their assistance to the Heroic Manager who has no need for the opinions of others because we possess all the answers.

Let me make it clear that there is typically nothing sinister in our motives. Most Heroic Managing results from a sincere, if misguided, desire to do what we think is best for the business. But we also do it because we like it. We enjoy feeling needed and are pleased to be able to help others resolve issues, find answers, and develop solutions. Everyone likes to feel important. It's a basic need in all of us, but for the Heroic Manager, that need manifests itself in ways that are unhealthy for the business.

Things often go from bad to worse as Heroic Managing becomes a self-reinforcing cycle. The manager creates an environment where people feel compelled to come to us for answers. The more often our people bring us problems to solve, the more irreplaceable we feel. The greater the number of times we are interrupted by knocks on the door, texts, and calls, the more important and valuable we feel. But as a Heroic Manager we can put our business into a spin, leading to an eventual business and emotional crash and burn.

Paths to Becoming a Heroic Manager

Aside from coveting the role of chief problem solver, there are other paths to becoming a Heroic Manager. Some simply lack the required skills. This is an all-too-common situation in business today.

In large organizations, people are typically promoted to leadership roles because they are very good at a skill or function. In a manufacturing facility, the most competent widget maker is often promoted to supervise the widget-making department. A company's most successful salesperson is likely to find themselves in charge of sales. The individual who seems to be most comfortable with customer interactions is promoted to customer service manager.

The problem is that the skills required to perform these functions has very little to do with managing people who perform these functions. Doing and managing are two separate and unrelated abilities. It can certainly be valuable for someone in customer service to understand the attributes of good customer service, but it's not essential. In fact, many management experts can make a strong case for the fact that a good manager needs no knowledge of the function they oversee. What's more important is that they know how to organize and monitor the work and ensure proper performance of subordinates.

This is what's known as The Peter Principle, a management concept published by educator Laurence J. Peter. As he pointed out, the concept ensures that people are promoted until they get to a job they can't do well. They rise to the level of their incompetence. New managers may have had tremendous hard skills but could have a complete lack of the soft skills (coaching, communication, performance management, etc.) that fill the management toolbox.

I've heard stories from frustrated new managers. They were naturally pleased to be recognized for their strong past performance, honored to be selected as a manager, and proud of the prestige and pay bump that accompanied the role. But they'd been tossed out of the comfortable nest of their functional role and expected to grow manager wings on their own.

For many people in the service industry, their management skills were acquired by watching how others managed or by how their previous managers managed them. This can be an effective way to acquire skills, but not always. In the case of entrepreneurs, many of us decided to strike out on our own precisely because we couldn't stand working for our previous managers. If this was because the managers were poor ones, then any skills we did pick up were probably poor as well.

Another path to Heroic Management is lack of trust, something all too common among entrepreneurs. When we launched our business, we literally had our hands on everything and were, in fact, the decider-in-chief. Then, as the business grew, we had to begin relying more and more on others, which is something that can feel quite unsettling.

Entrepreneurs find it hard to trust others with our baby, the business we brought into the world. Considering all the money, energy, and care put into starting it, it's understandable that we find it hard to trust others to make decisions about it. Talk about a trust fall! We are often afraid that our employees will drop the business on its head.

Consequences

Heroic Managing can kill a business primarily in two ways: stagnation and evacuation. The first invariably leads to the second.

Stagnation refers to fostering an environment where the presence of a chief problem solver in the organization becomes a bottleneck, significantly slowing activity. Nothing happens until the manager with the hero complex approves it. What should we do about Dave's repeated absences? How soon can we upgrade to the new and improved piece of equipment we need? How much can we spend on the company Christmas party? These and a thousand other issues must all be brought before the decider-in-chief to consider and resolve.

That makes for a lot of resolving, so the issues start stacking up like jets at LaGuardia on a snowy night. Employees are forced to wait for their audience with the Heroic Manager. Things that could, and should, be resolved in a matter of minutes can take hours or days. The company gets stuck in lower gear. Activity slows. Performance sags. Flexibility is lost. Customers wait too long for responses. Opportunities evaporate before they can be seized.

And then comes the evacuation. Employees head for the hills in search of a more productive work environment, especially the most energetic and dynamic ones. Their Heroic Manager's tight rein on decision making and problem solving creates an environment that's intolerable for those who are eager for opportunities and hungry to overcome challenges and take on more responsibility.

Employees feel less committed to company goals and responsibilities. They feel under-used, blocked, and have a lower sense of value to the company. Cynicism creeps in and employee morale deteriorates.

Who wants to stick around at a company where they don't feel challenged or allowed to grow by making decisions that affect their work? Heroic Managing forces the life out of a business by putting a stranglehold on employee development and squeezing the drive and initiative out of our people. How long would we put up with it if our boss never listened to our ideas or listened but never acted on them? Maybe we had that boss and that's why we started our own company.

Delegation is one of the premier approaches to employee development. By giving an employee the responsibility and authority to make decisions and take action on their own, they are forced to hone some critical business skills. Giving employees authority and responsibility increases their ability to assess a situation, develop solutions, identify the optimum course of action, and implement the solution. These are skills every owner and manager should want in all our employees.

Delegation requires some time and effort on our part, but there's a huge long-term payoff. While Heroic Managing creates a downward death spiral for companies, delegation creates powerful, upward energy. With each delegation, employees become more capable and able to take on ever-greater responsibility.

Some Heroic Managers, when faced with an overwhelming number of details that must be addressed, take a half step toward delegation. We offload some responsibilities and decision making to a trusted lieutenant, frequently a family member. Because we are both of one mind, we can have confidence that they will simply act the same way we would. If there's any uncertainty about what action to take, they understand that freelancing isn't advised and will just bring those uncertainties to the decider-in-chief.

The lieutenant does help speed up some decision making, but they also serve as a feeder system to the Heroic Manager. And we are right back where we started with one person making too many decisions and taking too long to make them, creating deep frustration among our employees.

Of course, not all employees will be frustrated to the point of evacuation. There will be many who stay, but in most cases our company would be better off if they left. The people who thrive in this top-down, command-and-control environment typically lack initiative. They either can't make decisions on their own because they were never shown how, they don't want to make decisions because when they do they get yelled at by the boss, or they just prefer to be told what to do. They are basically robots[16] doing the Heroic Manager's bidding.

If something unexpected or out of the ordinary happens, then activity comes to a halt. The robots aren't going to risk coming up with a solution or taking an action that hasn't been approved by the decider-in-chief. They ask for guidance, and if the answer is some time in coming, they are more than happy to shift into neutral and do nothing until they get clear guidance.

Strangling Our Business

In their book *Flight of the Buffalo*, authors James A. Belasco and Ralph C. Stayer write, "As the leader of my organization, I am responsible for creating the environment that enables each person to assume responsibility for his or her own performance. The people own the responsibility for delivering great performance. I am responsible for creating the environment where this ownership takes place."

It doesn't really matter what business we're in. At the end of the day, if we own or manage a company, we're in the people business. We might clean carpet, dry structures, install running tracks, distribute chemicals, sell software, or paint bridges. But these are just the products and services we sell. Our primary business is still people.

The literal bottom-line consequence of Heroic Managing is that it constrains our financial bottom line by smothering business development. It limits the growth of the business to the things the owner can control. Beyond that, Heroic Managing fails and the business becomes stalled.

As with many of the behaviors that form the Entrepreneurial Conspiracy, Heroic Managing can be insidious. The manager doesn't realize how their behavior is adversely affecting the organization. Employees are increasingly trained by experience to take no initiative or responsibility. Over time, the stress of taking responsibility for all that decision making may have the decider-in-chief railing in self-righteous indignation, "Can't anybody around here make decisions for themselves?! Do I need to do all the thinking?"

Well, yes, you do need to do all the thinking … until you decide to break the cycle.

Solutions

When you stop to think about it, we don't really sell our services to companies, we sell them to people. We don't have employees who work for us, we have people who work with us and families who depend on us. And we don't have investors who've bought into our company, we have people who've bought into our dream.

We aren't in a service business or a widget-making business; we are in the people business. Once we have this mindset, we can get to work creating an environment in our company that "enables each person to assume responsibility for his or her own performance," as Belasco and Stayer stated. Creating this environment starts with removing ourself from the role of chief problem solver in our company.

Here's the simplest self-assessment we can do to discover if we are a Heroic Manager. Ask ourself: "How many times a day do people in my organization come to me for help solving a problem or making a decision?" How often are we interrupted—in our office, by phone, or by email—by people needing questions answered or decisions made?

There's no absolute metric for a good answer to this question. It depends on a lot of things, including how long our company has been in business. In younger companies, when we're still sorting out the way things should work, we are required to make many decisions each day. It also depends on how our company is staffed. If we run very lean and the members of our team each wear many hats, everyone is likely to be seeking advice and help from one another frequently.

But as a general guideline for a typical business that's been around for a few years, if we have more than a half-dozen things brought to us each day for a decision, we may have become the decider-in-chief. If we are, here is a simplified version of the steps needed to correct the problem.

1. **Ask ourself why people are coming to us to deal with this problem or decision.** Do the people coming to us have the information needed to make a good decision? If not, should we be sharing more information with them? If they have the information and still come to us, then they obviously don't feel comfortable acting on their own. This means it's time for us to lighten our grip on the reins, encourage them to make more decisions, and let our employees help us drive the success of our organization.

2. **Delegate decisions to the people who have a stake in their outcome.** These are the people in the best position, with the strongest motivation, to make good decisions. If we've done the executive-level job of hiring the right people to start with, given them the information or resources they need, and developed them to their full potential, then we should have confidence that they'll make good decisions. The outcome won't always be perfect. They will make mistakes. That's part of learning and development. But over time, as their skills improve, we will be able to delegate ever-increasing responsibilities, freeing us to focus on other things ... or to focus on nothing and relax a bit.

3. **Follow up.** Notice that in point #2 it says delegate the decisions, not abdicate the decisions. When we do a good job of delegating, we schedule touchpoints throughout the delegated assignment and a final debrief. The best delegated assignments require employees to stretch their abilities and that means they could struggle or stumble. We need to be there to make sure they stay on course and successfully accomplish the assignment. And they need to hear from us that we recognize their accomplishment.

Delegate Well

As implied above, delegation isn't just handing off work to someone else. Delegation is a process that must be done correctly if we want to realize the benefits. Doing it wrong can actually create new problems.

Good delegation starts with identifying appropriate opportunities. Handing off some rote task that requires no decision making or initiative is assigning work, not delegating. Assigning work is certainly something that every supervisor and manager does routinely, but delegation requires handing off higher-level tasks.

It may be a one-time project or assignment or a permanent reassignment of some responsibility. It may be something that becomes part of the employee's job or things they could do to fill in when we're not available. The key is that the assignment must provide the employee with the chance to make decisions and build new skills that will expand their capabilities in the long run.

When delegating, one of the most difficult hurdles for Heroic Managers to overcome is being prepared to accept failure or under-performance. There is a good chance the person delegated the assignment will stumble and not do it perfectly or to the same level of quality that would be achieved if we were doing it ourselves. We must give them the freedom to fail without fear. If we can't live with that, and constantly struggle to find delegation opportunities where we can live with less-than-total success, then we shouldn't delegate and will need to resign ourselves to the fact that we are a Heroic Manager for life.

Will these mistakes cost the company money? More than likely. That's part of the cost of education. So there are two questions we want to ask ourselves. What can we do to reduce or eliminate any potential costs from these mistakes; and what is the company losing in lost opportunities and stalled growth because we're not delegating responsibilities to other people?

We also need to be prepared to devote additional time to managing the delegation. Don't expect to hand off an assignment, pat the employee on the head, and send them away to accomplish it without some help. We need to make it clear that we, or possibly someone else, will be available to help the employee overcome obstacles. The employee performing the new assignment may not move with speed or certainty, but they are building skills and gaining knowledge along the way and that takes some additional time.

If the employee does come to us for help or guidance, dial down the inclination to just give the easy answer. When they ask how to proceed, the best answer in most cases is another question: "What do you think?" Especially in organizations that have been under the direction of a Heroic Manager for some time, employees will be very tentative about making decisions or taking action. They are probably unsure about whether they truly have the authority to think and act.

Asking, "What do you think?" forces them to come up with solutions on their own. As they share those solutions with us, we can guide or shape them if necessary. We may not think their solution is the best solution, but unless the potential outcome would be disastrous or create serious problems, we should strive to let the employees try it their way. Knowing they own the decision will encourage them to really think it through. They know they will own the outcome as well, and while that can be a bit frightening, it is also tremendously empowering.

In the long run, asking, "What do you think?" forces employees to be more thoughtful, analytical, and creative. One of the consultants at my company remembers when he was a relatively new manager at a large company. He had a serious issue in one of his departments and was unsure how to proceed. He went to his superior, the vice-president of HR, to tell him about the problem and ask for direction. The vice president, an ex-Marine with a reputation for being tough, replied, "What do you think you should do?"

The young manager said he had no idea and that's why he was asking for help. The VP looked up with his face twisted in anger and thundered, "NEVER come to me with a problem until you have some possible solutions," and sent the manager on his way. It wasn't the most pleasant experience, but it made a lasting impression on the manager. It encouraged him to be more diligent in resolving issues and finding solutions, and he would quickly admit that it made him a better manager.

Delegate Effectively

Delegation isn't something that comes easy to many leaders, for several reasons. First is the fear that the employee can't do the assigned task. That's a valid concern. As I mentioned, good assignments should stretch the employee, and that means they may fail. We can minimize that risk by selecting the assignment carefully and being there to lend some guidance if necessary.

There's an opposite kind of fear. Some managers fear the employee will excel and do the job better than they could have. We should be so lucky! Wouldn't it be great to uncover some talent or skill in an employee, and then let them apply it to improving our business?

The other big stumbling block is that it takes time to delegate effectively. There's a process we need to follow, and it's not a set-it-and-forget-it proposition, as I mentioned earlier. There is almost no doubt that in just about every delegation situation, we could do it faster ourselves. But do we really want to always be doing it? Isn't it worth investing some time now to save time in the future?

A simple way to quantify the costs and benefits of a delegation, along with many other management actions, is to do what's called a 10-10-10 Analysis. This is where we consider the pros and cons of the delegation at three different time intervals of increasing length. The first interval should be 10 minutes, the here and now. The other two might be 10 days, weeks, months, or years, whatever we feel makes sense for the assignment being considered. The idea is that we look at the results in the short, medium, and long term. Let's run through a decision to see how it works.

Helen is responsible for arranging technical support for the computers and network in our company of eight people. She's been with the company for two years. We've been relying on Data Dan's to provide our IT support for about five years, but we aren't sure their techs are as current as they should be with technology or as responsive as we'd like when we call for emergency support. We wonder if it's time to change IT support providers.

We could do the investigation ourselves, but since Helen is responsible for arranging technical support, we are thinking about delegating the investigation to her. Should we?

What will the consequences be in the next 10 minutes, the short term?

On the con side, there's the time we will need to spend preparing to delegate the assignment. We need to think about the parameters. How much time should Helen spend on this? What are the metrics or traits of a strong IT support provider? Are there budget considerations? Thinking through these things and planning the delegation will take time.

Frankly, there aren't a lot of plusses yet. We can't be sure how Helen is going to respond. She could be thoroughly enthused at the opportunity to do the investigation. That would be a big boost to her morale and a nice plus. On the other hand, she could be feeling apprehensive about it. If this is one of the first things we've delegated, she could be really worried about doing a good job and concerned that she'll put in a lot of time and then we'll just do what we want to do anyway. Getting her over these concerns will require some reassurance and positive feedback.

What will the consequences be in the next 10 days, the medium term?

The cons here might include the fact that the delegation is taking Helen away from some of her regular work, which could put her behind on some deadlines. From our perspective, we probably need to devote some time to checking in on her progress to ensure she's on track.

On the plus side, odds are that she's pretty excited about this assignment. When people are working on things they enjoy, they are willing to put in some extra effort. There is a good chance that Helen will be willing to work extra hard on her day-to-day activities so they won't fall behind, meaning she will be more productive. For us, the plus is that we aren't spending our time doing the investigation. The time investment we need to make to support Helen is almost certainly less than what it would have taken us to do the investigation ourself.

What will the consequences be in the next 10 months, the long term?

At this point, the cons are likely behind us. In the long-term view, the only major con or risk is that Helen made a bad choice and we have to repeat the process. Of course, that could happen if we made the decision, too. It's hard to fully evaluate a service provider up front. We do our due diligence, and then hope they perform as expected. If it did turn out to be a bad choice, then another possible con is that Helen's confidence will have been shaken. The best solution is another delegation opportunity, perhaps one with a more assured outcome as a confidence rebuilder.

When we look at the plusses, they are many and they are important. In most cases, the outcome is positive and the employee successfully completes the delegation. Along the way, Helen has a chance to develop and use some new skills. She grows as an employee, making her a greater asset to our company. She becomes more engaged with the company. She feels like she plays a more important role than before, and she's more likely to stay with our company.

As the person who selected the new IT provider or decided to keep Data Dan's, she feels an increased responsibility to ensure that the relationship works and the services are up to par. People are always more committed to ensuring the success of decisions they made.

Our company should benefit because we have greater confidence in our IT support, and possibly even reduced downtime caused by IT issues.

An additional and significant plus for us is that we have time to devote to other things more important than investigating our IT support provider. A bigger plus is that we have a more engaged, energized, loyal employee.

The 10-10-10 Analysis is a simple but valuable tool that will help us put things into perspective. It will let us quantify the pros and cons of not only delegations, but many other management activities.

Dialing Down the Heroics

Increased delegation and giving employees greater responsibility and authority are at the heart of becoming a post-Heroic Manager. But there are a number of other things to be done to support and increase the effectiveness of those actions.

Surround ourselves with "A" players. This can be a fundamental hurdle for the Heroic Manager to overcome. We like being the hero. And one of the easiest ways to be the hero, to ensure that everyone must rely on us at every turn, is to hire employees who aren't as smart or capable as we are.

One of our consultants told me about his dating experience after his divorce. As a 30-something-year-old guy, he wanted to maximize his potential when it came to attracting ladies. He actually did some research on whether it was better to hang out with people who are better looking than you or not as good looking as you. He discovered that it was better to be seen with people less attractive because it would make you seem like the standout in the crowd.[17]

But running a business isn't dating. Before we can delegate with confidence, we need to get over our concerns about being outshone by others and ratchet up our talent pool. In the long run, that's what's best for our company. Without the right people on our team, we will be locked into our role as decider-in-chief.

We must learn to ask others for their input and advice. Again, this goes straight across the grain for Heroic Managers, but it's a critical step in engaging employees in the success of the business in a deeper way. They all want the business to succeed. Their income depends on it. But unless they're given the opportunity to offer input, they will simply wait for their manager to solve the problem, make the decision, or set the course.

There are four types of decision making: Autocratic, Consultative, Democratic, and Consensus. Autocratic is the go-to style for the Heroic Manager. In autocratic decision making, we decide. It's fast and easy, but based on all the negative outcomes of having a decider-in-chief running things, it should be clear why this isn't the best option.

Consultative is a step in the right direction. In this approach, we ask others for their input, but in the end, we make the decision. This is also a relatively fast and easy approach. And as long as we actually and demonstrably rely on that input in some of our decision making, this is a valid approach.

Democratic decision making can be a good approach but it's risky. We put the decision up for vote and agree to abide by the outcome. This can also be a relatively quick and easy decision-making style, but we need to exercise caution. If we're deciding what color carpet to use in the office or where to go for our team lunch, then democratic is a perfect choice. But typically we will not want to decide more consequential business decisions simply based on majority rule. Who wants to have a half-day every Friday? We do!!!

The post-Heroic Manager strives for consensus. To thrash out the path forward, we bring together the people in the best position to make the decision. Everyone has a voice, and everyone will own the decision, generating more enthusiasm in achieving its outcome. Because of the diverse input, the decision will also likely be the best choice. In the negative column is the fact that this is the slowest and most difficult approach. Consensus can be tough, and sometimes impossible, to reach. Still, if seeking consensus is a viable option, it should be the chosen option.

The value of employee input in decision making and completing delegated assignments will be greatly enhanced if we share information about the business with them. We shouldn't hold all our knowledge about the business close to our chest. We need to make it available to our employees. Tell them about the challenges we face and the opportunities ahead. Tell them how we're doing, where we're strong, and where we need to improve. And most importantly, be certain they understand how they fit into creating success for the business. If we want people to enthusiastically play our game, we must let them know what the rules are. And we need to let them know how they're doing and whether they and the company are gaining ground or losing ground.

When people have a deeper understanding about the business, they are able to make smarter decisions. When they understand their role in making the business stronger, they feel more engaged and excited about fulfilling that role to the best of their abilities. They will work harder, longer, and with more enthusiasm.

The Post-Heroic Manager

In order for their company to grow, the Heroic Manager must recognize this behavior and move beyond it by adopting the characteristics of the post-Heroic Manager. But doing so has risks.

When we increase our reliance on others to make decisions and take independent action, there's no doubt that we increase the chance of failure, although it's possible to minimize and manage the risk. Develop employees along a continuum of responsibility depending on the criticality of the assignment and the capabilities of the employee. Some employees may be capable of quickly taking on significant assignments, while others must be developed with much smaller baby steps of low-risk, low-complexity delegations.

Another risk is that our employees may outshine us in some areas. We will discuss this in the chapter on Swollen Ego.

In the short term, evolving to a post-Heroic Manager will require more time. In the early stages of delegation, we will need to take additional time preparing tasks for delegation, explaining them to the employee, and then supporting them with check-ins and answering their questions. Tasks will move more slowly as employees work through delegated tasks. But these are short-term effects.

In the long run, we are offloading assignments and freeing ourselves from the tyranny of the trivial. More work can be done, the work will get done faster, and we have additional time that can be used to do more in-depth strategizing ... or playing an extra nine holes.

We are also building a stronger, more loyal, committed team and a more resilient organization.

Some years ago, one of my clients was struggling with feeling the need to be the chief problem solver. He had just returned from a two-week visit overseas and expressed mixed emotions about the situation he found in his business when he got back. He told me that there were no big issues waiting for him. Problems and decisions hadn't piled up.

On the one hand, he felt a little uneasy because things had gone so well while he was away. He found he wasn't really needed to ensure the smooth operation of his business. But on the other hand, he felt satisfaction knowing he had done his job of developing the leadership talents in his people to the point where they could handle things on their own.

I told him I thought he was doing just fine in getting a handle on his chief problem solver problem.

CHAPTER 5
E-DRIFT

*D*rift is one of those verbs that can be both positive and negative. On the positive side, we talk about the fluffy, white clouds drifting through the sky. We relax as we drift down the lazy river, beverage in hand, at the resort hotel. We snuggle deep into the covers of our bed on a cold, winter evening and drift off to sleep.

The negative meanings come in references to losing our way. A ship drifts off course and is never seen again. In manufacturing, when a production machine drifts off tolerances, the result is typically scrap product. A long-time friend moves away and, despite our fervent intention to stay in touch, they slowly drift out of our life.

With entrepreneurs, there's another type of drift, and it falls into the negative category. I refer to this characteristic as Entrepreneurial Drift, or E-Drift for short (a nod to Michael Gerber's book *The E-Myth*). When a business owner seems to lose focus on their business and fails in their responsibility to provide stable, consistent, and positive leadership, it could be the result of E-Drift.

This isn't something we see only on an individual basis or microscale. The business landscape is littered with the names of companies, large and small, that have fallen victim to E-Drift. One of the most easily detected symptoms of E-Drift in an organization is when we go against our brand or nature and try to be something we aren't.

In working with business owners, I've witnessed many companies fall victim to the destructive effects E-Drift can have. I've seen it reduce once vibrant, profitable companies into shadows of their former selves, struggling to meet payrolls and threatened with insolvency.

We have all probably heard the frightening statistics about new-business failures. Only about 80% of new businesses survive to celebrate a year of operation. That was the case two decades ago and is still the case today. Survive is probably a good word, because I am sure that many struggled mightily to get past that one-year milestone, and more than a few owners took home truly paltry paychecks.

Take a look five years out and only half of those businesses are still operating. After 10 years, about one-third remain in business. Looking back over the decades, these statistics have remained remarkably consistent.

In my opinion, there is a statistic far more alarming than the failure rate of new businesses. You won't see it covered much in the business press and the statistics are hard to come by, but I have seen it firsthand. What I'm referring to is the number of companies that remain open but stall or languish for years. Their failure to thrive has nothing to do with the owners' IQ, prior business experience, or financial backing. Rather, it has to do with the ability of the owners to stay focused on the priorities needed to allow their company to gain traction and achieve the goals the owner had in mind at its launch. That's E-Drift.

I am the poster child for E-Drift. By nature, I am restless, constantly thinking about what I can do to make my business better and more profitable, always planning the next brilliant (at least in my own mind) step for my company. In some respects, I admire people who are able to do nothing. I can appreciate the peace and contentment they no doubt experience. But for me, doing nothing is just short of torture. My brain is constantly engaged, and I am typically in motion. This can be a good thing, but too often and for too many people, this constant motion is allowed to run wild.

When this happens, it becomes the unconstructive expression of the same creative energy and unbridled force that helped me launch my business. It's when we don't harness this energy and give it a positive direction that it dilutes our focus and undermines the growth of our company.

Before going any further, let me make it clear that I am not a psychologist, psychiatrist, or any other medical professional trained to make a clinical diagnosis of any behavioral condition. I simply have worked a long time with a lot of different business owners who struggled with trying to grow their company but got derailed time after time by their own behaviors—behaviors they often didn't recognize, but that caused them incredible frustration and brought damaging disruption to their company.

With that clarification, let's look at how can we can recognize E-Drift in our organization and in ourself.

Symptoms

E-Drift rarely starts by announcing itself with obvious erratic behavior. It doesn't grow in large and easily detectable stages. Like most of the behaviors engaged in the Entrepreneurial Conspiracy, it creeps slowly into our daily activities and progressively saps the energy of our organization.

Generally speaking, there are three types of E-Drift: Startup Business E-Drift, Successful Business E-Drift, and Bored Business E-Drift. While the causes are different, the symptoms can be similar.

Startup Business E-Drift

As a new business owner, it's unlikely that the business journey we began ended up at the precise destination we had planned. We had an idea about our business, what products or services we wanted to offer, how we planned to market them, what image we wanted to have in our service area, and so on. But there was much we probably didn't know yet. There were discoveries made along the way about our customers, our suppliers, the market, and our industry.

Based on these unfolding realities, we likely drifted off our intended course. We might have modified our services, our pricing, our promotional strategy. All these things represent alterations to our original business goals. All these deviations might have been valid and in the best interests of establishing the health and longevity of our business.

But these types of corrections go negative and begin to represent E-Drift when they become overly reactive and short-sighted. It's when we think an immediate response is required to every obstacle or unforeseen event that E-Drift begins to drag our business down. Making constant changes and continually altering or even reversing direction indicates that we are adrift.

Unfortunately, there is no metric or gauge that will tell us when we are making the appropriate changes to reestablish a sound course and when we are making erratic and excessive corrections that will have us chasing our own tail. As a startup, we may not have others in the business who we can rely on for their objective opinion. That can make the identification of E-Drift for new business owners particularly difficult to diagnose.

There are, however, a few easily recognized symptoms of E-Drift. One of them is being unaware of time. I can't tell you how often I've received phone calls late at night from new clients in startup businesses who were completely unaware of what time it was. I'll receive emails that are time-stamped at the wee hours of the morning. This isn't because it was the only time they had to write, but rather because they had completely lost track of time.

Another symptom I see a lot is impatience and frustration with the pace at which the staff is working. Owners can't understand why everyone doesn't move at the same frantic pace they do. The owner's self-talk includes: "Don't they understand that time is money? Don't they realize how much there is to do?! Why doesn't everybody else work 14-hour days? Where's their commitment?"

This can also extend to owner frustrations about how long it takes for projects to be completed by employees. Often, though, the delayed completions are the fault of the owner who couldn't take the time to completely define the project or provide the needed support.

Successful Business E-Drift

While Startup Business E-Drift is typically identified by behaviors, Successful Business E-Drift is often most easily identified by things; specifically, bright, shiny, new things. Based on the success of the business—success the owner feels they largely created single-handedly—they feel entitled to some well-deserved rewards.

The rewards could include new equipment, trucks, or buildings. In the owner's mind, these are things we are entitled to buy. And what's the big deal, anyway? The equipment can be written off as a business asset or expense, and as the owner, we are entitled to this kind of benefit, aren't we?

These purchases may, in fact, make perfect business sense. Too often, though, they are done in a knee-jerk manner with little thought given to their long-term implications. I see this a lot with newer business owners who have watched too many television shows about business success. Too often, the formula for these shows is a simple "risk followed by reward" scenario. And they all seem to have happy endings! This is the American success story of someone who takes an idea, makes it work, and profits mightily.

Of course, these shows tend to focus on the successes, especially the grandest successes. Complex problems are solved in 30 minutes (actually less after deducting the time for commercials). They are called reality shows, but there's little that's real about how they portray what's required to make a business a success. While these shows make good television, they are terrible at preparing entrepreneurs for the reality of starting and running a business.

Some owners feel that it's appropriate and actually beneficial to surround ourselves with the trappings of success. We think this will convey to customers that we are successful and therefore someone who is obviously very good at what we do. That may be true, particularly in some businesses and in some instances. But it is usually not the case.

The well-known symbol of success for Mary Kay cosmetics sales consultants, for example, is a pink Cadillac.[18] It serves as a powerful and tangible symbol of sales success to everyone who sees it. Considering that the company is based on multi-level marketing and must attract a constant stream of new recruits, the cars are no doubt a powerful incentive for people to join the Mary Kay team. These luxury cars definitely drive success for the employees and the company. That's not an example of E-Drift.

If we hire a realtor to sell our home, we might be impressed to see them drive up in a shiny new Lexus. That demonstrates that the realtor is good at selling homes and will probably be able to sell ours. Again, that's not E-Drift.

On the other hand, if we are on the buying side, we are less likely to feel good about the realtor making a lot of money because that's going to be our money making the payment on that car.

Another example demonstrating how flashy vehicles can create problems for us comes from an article written by Ruth King in the publication "Contractor Cents." In it, she described something she called the "Mercedes Benz Syndrome." The article relates the situation of a business owner meeting with a potential investor about a cash infusion for the owner's business. When the investor saw the expensive car the owner was driving, he had doubts about the owner's actual need and opted not to put money into the business.

For most businesses, especially small businesses, showing up at a customer's house or business in an expensive vehicle is probably not the smartest move. The customers won't be impressed by the fact that we've charged other people enough to drive a car fancier than what most people can afford.

That luxury car may also not present a good image at work. The majority of employees would like being paid more than what they receive now. In discussions with their boss about an increase, the conversation often includes reasons why a big raise, or any raise, is not possible: the need to control costs, to put money back into the business, and doing what's in the best long-term interests of the company. That's hard to square with the fact that the boss parks a Ferrari out front. And having a prominent spot near the door reserved for the owner's car throws salt in the open wound.

This isn't always the case, of course. There are business owners who treat their employees well and compensate them fairly. In some cases, employees are pleased to see their hardworking and much-loved leader reward themselves with that luxury vehicle. In most cases, though, displays of wealth are more likely to garner backlash than pats on the back.

Even if the expense for our new toy is very small compared to the revenue generated by our business, we must consider what they refer to in politics as the "optics." If my state, Ohio, was in the middle of some horrible disaster, and the governor had been working around the clock for two days to do everything he could to help, but a photographer catches him taking a five-minute break with a beer in his hand, that's an example of bad optics. The facts don't matter. What people see and how they react to it does. And it could change the image that customers, employees, and investors have of us and our business.

Bored Business E-Drift

In this form of E-Drift, success breeds complacency. We've done everything right and our business is thriving. Our recruiting and development efforts have paid off, providing us with a superb team of energized and capable individuals. We've done so well at organizing our business that it almost runs itself. We can be gone for days or even weeks at a time and our business operates without a hiccup. We don't get urgent emails or phone calls asking what we want the team to do, and when we return, there's no pile of folders that require our immediate action. Our days are predictable and fairly routine.

Sounds blissful, right? For some people, maybe, but not for many small business owners. Some of us tend to enjoy near-frantic activity levels rather than the day-to-day, routine responsibilities of running a business. We miss the stimulation of unraveling tough problems and dealing with the latest crisis. It's contrary to our nature to not be actively engaged in the business. We feel a bit lost and maybe even unneeded. So, our active minds go in search of something to do and E-Drift begins.

We poke our noses into things where our noses probably don't belong. Maybe we think it's time to refresh our website and take that on as a personal assignment. We always wondered how websites work. This is the perfect opportunity to find out.

Maybe it's time for a new advertising campaign, something we'd really enjoy working on. Advertising sounds fun, and we have some great ideas for a new campaign.

Isn't it time to rearrange work areas? We saw some simple CAD software for home design that we were thinking about buying for our family room remodel. Redesigning our office space will be a swell project to practice on the software before doing our home job.

We take our eyes off the routine ,and sometimes boring but very important, things we should be doing. We start frittering away our time on projects that are someone else's responsibility or that should be delegated to someone better suited and capable of accomplishing them. We do things that distract us from what we should be doing. Our responsibilities, while they may be routine, are still essential to operations. If we're doing something else, then those things probably aren't getting done.

The people who should be doing those things are likely to become frustrated and resentful. They really don't want or appreciate us dabbling into their responsibilities, but they certainly aren't going to tell us that. Instead, they will suffer and seethe in quiet.

Another and more serious symptom is when the bored owner looks for excitement outside the company. Just like the bored spouse who looks outside the marriage for something stimulating, this is likely to turn out badly. Often, the object of this new enthusiasm is typically business expansion, perhaps taking the business into new and uncharted terrain.

The owner looks at the success the company had in its original territory and sees geographic expansion to another, comparably sized market as the path to doubled sales. That may turn out to be true, but the expansion shouldn't be pursued based on the idea that if we did good here, then going there will help us do even better. That's a bit like saying if an ounce of cleaning agent cleans well, then two ounces will be twice as good!

This form of E-Drift is especially dangerous when we consider business ventures that are completely unrelated to our core business. We are drawn by the promise of big bucks and the excitement of the new venture. There will, no doubt, be excitement, but too often it's like the thrill felt when falling off a cliff as both the energy and financial reserves of our primary business are drained away in support of the new venture.

Successful entrepreneurs are typically innovators, eager and open to new ways of doing things. Bored business owners might find themselves chasing things down rabbit holes. It's possible they will actually catch a rabbit, but more often they will simply find themselves in a hole.

Loss of Focus

The common symptom of all three causes of E-Drift is difficulty sustaining attention on a task or following through on a project until it's complete. Frequently, this inattention is the result of distractions that grab our attention and refuse to let go. These distractions don't have to be big. They can be as basic as a phone call, a visitor to the office, or a question from an employee. Anything at all.

No matter how serious we are about trying to follow through on a project, the minute a distraction shows up, we're off and running after it. Like a dog chasing a car, it's instinctive. The dog isn't sure why it's going after the car and wouldn't know what to do with the car if it caught it, but it can't resist the chase. Owners with E-Drift jump from project to project completely unaware of the disruptive effect this can have on our staff or the impact our frequent shifts of attention can have on the time demands of our employees.

As we learn more about E-Drift, we may be struck by its similarity to Blurred Vision. In fact, there is quite a bit of overlap in the symptoms and causes. There is, however, a significant difference, and that drives different consequences and solutions. People who suffer from Blurred Vision behave erratically and move without purpose because we fail to plant a stake in the ground. We don't establish clear strategies and goals, and we waste energy due to our unfocused efforts. Those who suffer from E-Drift, on the other hand, drive too many stakes and do not drive any of them very deep. Either way, we are unable to focus on anything for very long and fritter away our time and talent on unfocused and unproductive activities.

E-Drift is similar in many ways to attention deficit hyperactivity disorder, ADHD. The symptoms of both include excitability, hyperactivity, impulsivity, difficulty focusing, a short attention span, and swings between boredom and excitement. The risk in identifying some of the symptoms of ADHD in a business owner or manager is that we might be viewed as somehow lacking or inferior in our role. This would be a huge mistake. I have worked with many owners exhibiting these traits, but they were also highly intelligent, creative people with strong business instincts who were successful in spite of their ADHD tendencies.

Awareness of ADHD-like behaviors and their relation to E-Drift will help business owners, as well as the people who work for us, identify the potentially negative behaviors and control or channel them in positive ways.

Causes

We are naturally predisposed to being affected by E-Drift. By "we," I mean people like you and me who launched and work in small businesses. I have no statistics to support it, but I believe the percentage of owners with ADHD-like symptoms is higher in small businesses than it is for those who work at larger businesses.

Small businesses, and service businesses in particular, are perfect playgrounds for people with these traits. Small businesses offer lots of large motor activity, sketchy accountability, and frequent changes of scenery. Who needs caffeine to get revved up when you can own a small business?!

Those traits are, in part, what drove many of us to set out on our own. When controlled and properly directed, those traits are also what drives entrepreneurs to success. The short attention span, easily distracted, hyperactive personality represents the characteristics of many small business owners. It seems a lot of entrepreneurs are genetically hardwired with this condition.

If we're honest with ourselves, many of us would probably admit that one of the driving forces behind starting our own business was that we made a lousy employee. The work we were doing wasn't stimulating enough to keep us excited and interested ("Oh, for Pete's sake, please don't make me do that one more time!"), so we quit. Or, our bosses weren't willing to put up with our inconsistent performance or lack of follow-through on projects, so they decided the future of our employment for us with a two-word interjection, "You're fired!" In response, we decided "I'll show them!" and went off and started our own business.

In many cases, this is a good thing. But what we often fail to take into account is that the behaviors that led to our departure from our previous jobs didn't mysteriously disappear when we started our own business. We brought them with us! Only now, these behaviors are greatly magnified. Instead of being one cog in a large machine, we are the main cog in a smaller machine, and our behavior has a far greater impact on the organization. When we don't recognize these behaviors and address them, we frequently doom ourself and our company to running around in circles year after year—feeling busy all the time but never really getting ahead.

Early in my consulting career, I did a survey and found that 40% of my clients were actually diagnosed with ADHD. They were in a large-motor activity business where they got to drive from site to site and spend their days doing hands-on work. The service business is a great fit for people like those clients. They love working hard and breaking a sweat. But trying to get them to stay focused and follow through on things can be a challenge.

Let's return to our three types of business drift and look at some other, more detailed causes, beginning with Startup Business E-Drift.

Startup Business E-Drift

In an effort to find the right course to get their fledgling operation off to a good start and on the way to long-term profitability, the new business owner constantly makes corrections and adjustments. They modify their (probably vague) business plan on the fly and repeatedly refine or redirect their service and business processes. This is necessary and appropriate, but it can also be exhausting and futile.

I got a small, remote-control quadcopter as a gift. It's the kind you fly around in your living room while trying to avoid crashing into lamps and annoying your family and pets. In addition to the basic speed, direction, and altitude controls, there were also two levels of control sensitivity: beginner and skilled. In beginner mode, the controls were simply less responsive. Mashing a control stick the whole way to its limit would cause the drone to gently move in that direction. With the sensitivity set to skilled mode, the same control action would send the drone zooming dramatically in that direction.

The reason for the two levels of control is that new pilots, whether flying toy quadcopters or full-size planes, tend to overcontrol.[19] Any down motion of the plane is met with a fast and excessive pull-back on the controls to bring the nose up. Because the newbie pilot overcontrolled, the next step is usually an equally fast but less excessive push forward on the controls. The cycle repeats in successively smaller corrections until level flight is achieved. The resulting flight path is anything but smooth and, for anyone unfortunate enough to be a passenger, likely to require an air-sickness bag.

As new business owners we also have the tendency to overcontrol and the result on our employees is similar to what is experienced by the passengers of new pilots. Because of our lack of business exposure, it's hard to know how soon and how much to respond to the many challenges faced while getting the business metaphorically airborne. The resulting ride can be disorienting to employees, investors, and family members. Assuming we make more good corrections than bad, we will begin to develop the insight and skills needed to more delicately and prudently adjust our course.

With an owner who suffers from E-Drift, this constant and dramatic changing of direction never ends. In fact, as the company grows it sometimes gets worse because we now have additional cash to throw at these directional changes. Regardless, the effect on our employees is the same: motion sickness and exhaustion.

Successful Business E-Drift

While seeking an optimum business course, new business owners have no time to think about fancy toys and other potential paybacks for our hard work. We are frequently cash strapped and struggling to make payroll, so we aren't thinking about a new car; we are focused on the single most important task at hand—survival!

It's when we've established our business and have a steady income that Successful Business E-Drift is likely to happen. As the coffers start to fill and our balance sheet gets healthier, we have time to consider some personal extravagances. We start flirting with the trappings of success. We drift toward the feel-good rather than the effective.

Dr. Dieter Zetsche, former CEO of German carmaker Daimler, spoke for a lot of business owners when he said, "We get stupid when we start succeeding." Unfortunately, the good doctor knew what he was talking about.

After watching many businesses struggle for years before finally making the transition from money-losing gambles to money-making businesses, I'm convinced that the greatest threat to a business doesn't exist when the company is strapped for cash. Rather, it's when the company is making money. When a company is losing money, it's easy for the owners to stay on task. There's nothing that gets a business owner's attention like losing money. It's when we start to become successful and have both the money and the extra time to think about how to spend it that we start getting in trouble.

Bored Business E-Drift

And finally, let's explore the causes of Bored Business E-Drift. It happens when running the business becomes routine. Let's face it, most entrepreneurs are charter members of the "once-and-done" club. After we develop the skills, talent, and experience to successfully do something, we become bored and start looking for the next exciting thing to capture our attention. The daily routine becomes a daily grind. Rather than following through with a project until it has time to mature and produce the results we need, our insatiable quest for an adrenaline rush propels us to prematurely move on to the next new thing.

Again, our nature as entrepreneurs is to get bored with the status quo. This is something we regularly see with our clients.

Consequences

Startup Business E-Drift

As an owner experiencing Startup Business E-Drift, the most common consequence is exhaustion for us, our employees, and possibly our suppliers and other business associates as well. An owner and their business have a lot in common with a party balloon that is blown up and then released without tying the neck. It frantically zooms this way and that way until the air is gone and it flops to the ground, literally out of gas. When we are constantly changing our business priorities or direction, it drains the time, energy, and resources of us and our people.

The good people we hired aren't likely to hang around. No doubt they were excited to get in on the ground floor of our young company. But instead of riding an elevator that would take them up to bigger and better things, it feels more like a trip on Disney's Tower of Terror that simply jerks them up and down. They want to help build the business. They want us and our company to succeed. But in the face of constantly changing assignments and expectations, they feel their work is wasted and that it's pointless to do their best. It's better to take their talents elsewhere.

Unless we can get our Startup Business E-Drift under control, our business could face the same fate as that party balloon.

Successful Business E-Drift

When businesses stop simply surviving month to month and start making money, lots of things change. As the owner, we finally feel like we can calm down a bit and breathe. We experience the elation of positive cash flow and a better bottom line. We move from panic mode to maintenance mode. While this is all wonderful and a stage of business that every owner aspires to, it also opens the door to the danger of Successful Business E-Drift.

This usually happens in bits and pieces rather than major and obvious changes. It's a gentle transition rather than an abrupt shift and it typically begins with business-related purchases. It might start as a crapshoot on an interesting but untried and unproven new advertising scheme. Maybe we come across some cool, cutting-edge piece of equipment in a trade magazine and decide we'd like to have one to give it a try. These small purchases are gateway drugs to ever bigger and more costly purchases that are ever harder to understand and impossible to justify.

The drift accelerates and takes a nasty turn when the purchases shift from true, if illogical, business expenses to toys. The most dangerous form of E-Drift happens when the owner of the business feels entitled to taking some personal rewards and begins flirting with the trappings of success. This is where we drift toward what feels good and away from what's effective.

Don't take this to mean that I am against realizing some tangible benefits from the success we created for ourself and others. There's nothing wrong with rewarding ourself for the sacrifice and hard work we've put into our business. As someone who's been there, I know we deserve rewards for what we do and what we have accomplished. The ability to build financial success, and the physical rewards it enables us to obtain, are part of the reason we launched our business in the first place.

What I'm talking about is when an owner starts plundering the company treasury to finance the trappings of success. The huge mortgage payments. The expensive luxury cars. The unplanned and unnecessary equipment purchase. These drifting owners are gambling with their company's future success and the livelihood of their employees to finance a successful appearance. These activities and purchases can become distractions from the very activities that produced success in the first place.

An insurance adjuster once commented to me about how frequently he sees boats, motorhomes, and other motorized toys sitting in the warehouses of small business owners he visits. You get the impression some service company owners measure their success by how many cylinders they own. The adjuster said that although it's not his place to question the business owner's purchases, it does make him question their invoices the next time they cross his desk. You can be sure it has a similar effect on the people who work for an owner who denies employees raises or makes them work with outdated or broken equipment.

The heart of our consulting business is helping our clients become more successful in their businesses. When working with clients exhibiting Successful Business E-Drift, our job becomes much more difficult. Clients who are struggling know they need help and are eager for our advice. But when the client's problems are the result of being successful, it's often hard for them to see the problem. Their blindness to the issue is made worse by the fact that many of them see their purchases not as an extravagance but rather as an entitlement. The recommendations from our advisors to owners in the throes of Successful Business E-Drift frequently fall on deaf ears.

Bored Business E-Drift

The bored business owner fondly looks back on our start-up days, peering through rose-colored glasses on the struggle to build the business and reliving the elation of establishing it as a successful and profitable enterprise. Those were the good old days. Now that enterprise has lost its luster, tarnished by the routine nature of operating a well-staffed and well-run company. We are seduced by the idea of setting off on a new business venture that promises fresh challenges, excitement, and wealth.

There certainly are people who successfully jump from business venture to business venture, creating additional wealth at each jump. Yet for every wealthy serial entrepreneur, there are far more of us who built a bridge too far. We overreached, overextended, and ended up overwhelmed. We delved into ill-advised ventures that failed, wiping out the progress and wealth we built in our previous, successful business.

In his book *How the Mighty Fall*, author Jim Collins writes about the second stage of business decline, something he calls "The Undisciplined Pursuit of More." This is where a business owner rationalizes that if we have a reasonably successful business operating in one location, we should be much more successful by having five locations. On paper this seems to make perfect sense: one times one is one; and five times one is FIVE!

The reality is that the geographic expansion of service businesses often fails because we woefully underestimate the need for the two most precious resources to make the expansion succeed: cash and competent people. The cash component is pretty straightforward: we'll need more than we planned on. Jim Collins addresses the people issue head-on when he writes, "When an organization grows beyond its ability to fill its key seats with the right people, it has set itself up for a fall."

Solutions

E-Drift comes in several forms and may attack our business during the early stages, once we've built it into a success, or after it's running so smoothly and profitably that it requires little attention from us. But at every stage, there are countermeasures and solutions we can take to limit or eliminate the pernicious effects of E-Drift.

Start-Up Business E-Drift

The solution for Start-Up Business E-Drift is simple to state but difficult to implement. We must be sure to have a plan and then stick with it. Not just a plan in our head; we need to have a written business plan. Entrepreneurs are famous, or more correctly we are infamous, for waxing eloquent to anyone who will listen about all the things we're going to accomplish with our business. Those are dreams, not plans, until they are committed to paper.

Our plan doesn't need to be fancy or complicated. In fact, the simpler it is, the more likely it is that we will follow it. But it does need to be written down. The act of writing it forces us to think more deeply about our intentions and aspirations, and to crystalize and capture them in concrete words. The other benefit of writing it down is that it lets other people have a look at it.

Now when we come across a new opportunity or obstacle, before responding—and possibly over-responding—we should take another look at our plan. Consider whether it is really necessary to change course or if we should adhere to the original plan. If we have surrounded ourself with strong, competent people they can help with this evaluation. They have a big stake in our business's success, and they will probably be able to make a more-objective assessment of the situation. They can help us decide whether we need to stick to the plan or modify it.

This deliberate approach to addressing problems and opportunities will help minimize overreactions, saving ourself and our organization considerable stress and conserving our scarce resources. After careful evaluation, we may determine that a change to the plan is absolutely in order. If we're sailing a ship that's on course to crash onto some rocks, then it's certainly a good use of our resources to adjust the sails and steer to safer waters. But we don't need to change course every time there's a shift in the wind or waves.

Many new business owners make a habit of multitasking. There is so much to do that the only way to accomplish everything seems to be doing more than one thing at a time. It's an appealing idea. Many of us pride ourselves on our ability to multi-task. Science, however, tells us that we'd be better off single-tasking.

According to a recent *Forbes* article,[20] it turns out that 98% of the population doesn't multitask very well. The 2% who are good at it are true supertaskers, but they aren't like most normal humans. The rest of us aren't really multitasking at all, because we aren't doing more than one thing at a given time. What we are, in fact, doing is shifting back and forth from one task to another.

The loss of efficiency when attempting to multitask is obvious. When we shift between tasks, it takes our brain time to refocus and the effects on productivity are huge. Studies show that multitasking can reduce productivity by as much as 40%. Wouldn't we all like to be 40% more productive? Of course, but how to do that? Here are some suggestions.

Start each day with a list of the things we need, or at least hope, to accomplish. If we want to attempt an even-deeper level of self-control, we can also decide how much time to spend on each task on the list. Then set aside blocks of time for specific activities. Whether it's invoicing, marketing, training, conducting a meeting, or whatever, assign a time limit to it. Our to-do list must also include some open blocks of time when we can address the unplanned issues that inevitably pop up every day. But we shouldn't use unplanned issues as an excuse for not having a plan in the first place.

It can be helpful to share our to-do list with others. Some people are very self-disciplined and can stick to their to-do list on their own. Most of us benefit from knowing that others are aware of how our day is scheduled. Sharing the list has the added benefit of letting people know when they should plan to come to us with their issues or questions. Rather than interrupt us when we're deep in thought and churning through one of our scheduled tasks, they are more likely to appear at our door at the time we set aside to address unplanned issues and tasks.

Now, as we use the list to guide our actions for the day, we should give ourself the small but genuine satisfaction of checking things off as we accomplish them. At the end of the day, hopefully we will have achieved the highest priority items, which are those we thought were most important that day to move our business forward.

There will, of course, be days when our list is quickly shredded by unforeseen, critical items that must be dealt with. In most cases, though, things that occur during the day can wait. Rather than repeatedly shifting between tasks, we should focus on one at a time and be careful not to let urgent items overpower the critical items. By following this plan, our productivity will improve significantly.

Successful Business E-Drift

How best to resist the siren song of a sweet new vehicle, the latest and greatest piece of equipment, or some other extravagant purchase? By dialing down our enthusiasm for the purchase long enough to ask ourself three questions.

1. **What is the business outcome of this purchase?**
   The importance of this question is obvious when thinking about new equipment or facilities for our company. It may be less obvious for the toy we want to buy for our personal benefit, but we still need to consider how it will affect the business. Is the expense large enough that it will have a negative effect on the company's finances? How will our employees, customers, and other business associates respond and feel about the

purchase? We might say it's none of their business and that may be true, but we shouldn't ignore the optics of the purchase—how it's viewed by others. They'll probably have a response, and we need to think about whether that response is in the best interests of the business.

2. **Will this purchase add value to our customers?**

Obviously, this rules out the Prevost motorhome we were thinking about unless, of course, we plan on using it to shuttle customers to sporting events and make it the base of operations for tailgating. Even if that is the plan, see the next question.

The benefit to customers may be indirect but still real. Improvements that primarily affect our employees will, or certainly should, enable them to provide better service or to operate more efficiently. That, in turn, provides a benefit to our customers.

3. **Will the expected return justify the investment, not only of our money but also our time and energy?**

When it comes to equipment or facilities, doing a cost-benefit analysis for each planned equipment purchase is Business 101 stuff. New, cool, and sexy aren't good reasons to buy equipment. The ability to provide better service to our customers and make more money is the only good justification. Will our employees think "Brilliant purchase!" or "What the heck were you thinking?"

I recall working on a business plan with a client in the Southwest. At one point, the owner pulled me aside to let me know that he thought his company was in real trouble. The best way for me to quickly assess the health of a company is to look at its financial statements, so I took a quick look at his. It was blindingly apparent that the company was beyond being in trouble. It was dead, but no one had told it to fall into the grave yet.

One line item in particular stood out as an example of how he'd gotten himself into trouble. His P&L showed a $20,000 expense to Mr. Harley. I asked the owner what service or product he'd purchased from Mr. Harley that cost so much. He looked at me without batting an eye and said, "Dude, that's my Harley." A classic example of Successful Business E-Drift. While I didn't respond with the words that immediately came to mind, I did explain that the first step to digging himself out of the hole he'd gotten into was to sell the Harley.

Bored Business E-Drift

The cure for Bored Business E-Drift is also dependent on asking ourselves a question. As we sit at our desk thinking about some new direction, diversification, or major expansion, we should ask "Will it make me a fortune?"

That was a question posed to 33-year-old me by one of the first consultants I hired for my fledgling business. I had the opportunity to buy a supply company. I could have purchased it for pennies on the dollar of its market value. The owner simply needed to quickly get out of the business. I asked my new consultant if I should buy it. He never asked me about markets, margins, upside, or any of that. He asked me if the business was going to make me a fortune. I asked him why, and he said, "Because it's going to cost you a fortune. It will cost you in time, it will cost you in focus on your primary business, and it will cost you in relationships because you'll be devoting too much time to it."

To this day, that remains some of the best business advice I've ever received.

In most cases, we will need to rely on the cash, talent, and resources of our current business to support a new venture. Does it have the strength to carry that load? What's going to happen to the core business when it becomes the energy source for our next big thing?

Instead of investing the time and money in launching a new venture, would we be better off focusing the same time, money, and energy on the business we already know? It's not as fun or as interesting, but it's probably a lot smarter. It is far more prudent to seek new challenges and increased wealth by building on our original success through carefully considered growth and expansion of the existing business.

The siren song of a new venture can be sweet and compelling. When clients come to us with ideas that would take them far from their core business, we encourage them to think about the competitive advantage they would gain. Following a clear-headed analysis, we usually arrive at some classic, old-time advice: stick to your knitting. Stay focused on what you know, and look for ways to grow from the base of your existing business and services.

If the prospect of blooming where we're planted leaves us feeling demoralized and depressed, maybe it's time to cash out of the business. We aren't doing the business any good and are probably eroding the value we will eventually realize from it. Get out while the getting, and the money, is good.

We constantly hear about people reinventing themselves. Maybe that's just what we should do. Find something that fascinates us. Find something to challenge us.

Find something to enrich our life. But we shouldn't do it at the expense of our current business and the employees who helped us build it into a success.

E-Drift behaviors aren't all bad. After all, they frequently represent versions of the same characteristics or traits that encourage entrepreneurs to launch our business in the first place. It's that constant, nagging dissatisfaction with the status quo, that endless need to tweak things to make them better, that restlessness that compels one to explore new things. Like other behaviors that make up the Entrepreneurial Conspiracy, the behaviors that represent E-Drift can be used in positive ways.

It requires a concerted effort and constant vigilance to make sure we don't let our behaviors turn negative and morph into E-Drift. We must channel the energy and creativity that can lead to E-Drift and use it to grow our company and achieve the dreams that were the reason we went into business in the first place.

CHAPTER 6
HIDING OUT

We are now on the fifth of the six behaviors that comprise the Entrepreneurial Conspiracy. The final two behaviors—Hiding Out and Swollen Ego—are doubly dangerous. That's because each of them has its own unique, debilitating effects on a business, but they also do the added damage of the previous four behaviors by masking them, making them more difficult to detect.

Owners and managers guilty of hiding out lose touch with their business and are therefore unlikely to notice the symptoms of the preceding behaviors. Their business could be speeding toward a cliff, while the owner is in the backseat reading a book, clueless to the coming catastrophe.

A different car analogy might better illustrate Hiding Out. Imagine being behind the wheel of your car or truck and driving without the benefit of instruments on the dashboard. No speedometer, no fuel gauge, no temperature, no oil pressure. How long could you safely operate your car like this? Eventually, you will get pulled over for speeding, run out of gas, or burn up the engine due to lack of oil or coolant.

This scenario represents an owner who has simply lost touch with their business. In the worst cases of Hiding Out, the owner is nearly oblivious to what's going on with their business. In addition to having no gauges to keep them informed about the health of the business, it would be like also having the windshield spray-painted black, so they have no idea where the business is headed. In this scenario, the amount of time the business will continue safely on course without a calamity is significantly shorter.

The number of owners who are actively hiding out from their financial data, one of the most-common indications of this behavior, is staggering. Rather than learning how to understand our numbers, most owners abdicate this responsibility by saying things like, "I'm not a numbers guy. I'm better with the hiring or advertising." Or, "I must be making money, I'm paying the bills (or I still have checks left in the checkbook!)." Allowing ourselves to think this way is a lot like playing Russian Roulette. We can't dodge that bullet forever. The gun will eventually go off and our business will be mortally wounded.

How do we recognize if we are hiding out? Let's look at some of the symptoms.

Symptoms

My introduction to the concept of business owners hiding out came early in my consulting career, when I was working with a commercial construction contractor. This particular contractor had tons of trucks and heavy equipment and dozens of employees. Being in commercial construction in a northern climate, the company's work season pretty much wrapped up by early December when the weather delayed projects until the spring thaw.

Ignoring Financial Data

Like most construction businesses, the company's cash flow usually felt very one-way, and not the good way. Cash mostly seemed to flow out rather than in, and their margins were paper thin. In talking with the owner, it was clear that his evaluation of the company's cash flow situation was based purely on his gut feeling. The company didn't really track their numbers throughout the year. It wasn't until the end of the year, or sometimes early in the following year when their accountant got into their books, that he had a solid idea of whether or not the company had made any money. That's no way to manage a business!

As I worked with more and more companies and their owners, I discovered this behavior was not all that unusual. When I'd ask to look at their books, these Hiding Out owners always had some rationale for why they couldn't be produced. I'd hear comments like, "Oh, yeah, we're still working on them" or "We haven't closed out last year yet" (and this is in June!). In some cases, I'd see a look on their face similar to what you'd see on the young boy with frosting all over his shirt after being asked, "Did you eat the piece of cake we saved for your sister?!"

The owners of the commercial construction company I mentioned worked like crazy all year long in the hope of making money, but they had no knowledge of how well they were performing financially on a monthly or quarterly basis. They were flying financially blind, often ending up in a place they didn't want to be—in the red.

One of the most painful things for me to see at a company is an owner who's working very hard and has an energized team supporting them, but they continue to lose money. This is often the case because, when absent good financial data, they just relentlessly toil away with no idea whether all that work is generating a profit. They could be losing money on a certain service, so the more of it they sell, the faster they go into the red. You won't stay in business long if you're losing money on the services you deliver while deluding yourself that you'll make it up in volume.

Early the following year, when the accountant would get their hands on the books to do tax preparation, the owners finally got the lowdown on how they'd done the prior year. Regardless of the verdict, the owners were never pleased. If they had lost money, they would be emotionally crushed, wondering how they could have worked so hard and not made any money. Then they became stressed, wondering if they would still be in business the following year. If they had made money, the owners' responses weren't much better. "If we made all this money, where is it!? Where's the cash?" they'd cry. "And now the government wants their cut?!" There is no winning for a Hiding Out owner when it comes to their financials.

There are two flavors of failing to monitor our financials. The Hiding Out owner is guilty of willful ignorance. They intentionally avoid digging into the numbers, for reasons we will explore in a minute. But there are also owners who genuinely don't see the importance of staying on top of their company's financials. This could be the result of Blurred Vision or No Accountability rather than Hiding Out. Regardless of the cause, it has the potential to be disastrous.

The statement that "I'm just not a numbers guy" is a poor excuse. Every business owner needs, to some extent, to be a numbers guy. If we genuinely don't have the ability to look at our financial data and identify the appropriate responses, then we had better quickly get a numbers guy on our payroll or start planning for a going-out-of-business sale.

Ignoring Other Performance Measures

Ignorance of our company's financial performance is probably one of the most obvious and serious symptoms of Hiding Out, but it is not the only one. There are other performance metrics that must also be monitored to ensure the strength and longevity of our company. That includes the list of key performance indicators (KPIs) that require the owner's attention. Consider some of the time-related KPIs, such as how long it typically takes to complete a job, how long it takes to process documents, and how long it takes to get paid.

Consider KPIs related to money. How much does the average job bring in? What are the typical costs for a job? Are some types of jobs consistently more profitable than others?

One more category of KPIs is the metrics related to quality. What is the average rating our customers give us on the various services we provide? What percent of jobs result in angry or dissatisfied customers?

Every one of those KPIs, and dozens more, could be critical to the success of a company. They each require a system to collect and analyze the data, identify the most critical opportunities for improvement, and develop and implement appropriate corrective action. But for the Hiding Out owner, these performance metrics go unnoticed or ignored.

Avoid Conflict and Confrontation

The Hiding Out manager will go to great lengths to avoid being involved in or having to resolve conflict. I believe most people are conflict avoiders. We prefer harmony, and we abhor having to deal with conflict. I believe entrepreneurs are particularly timid when it comes to conflict. We like doing nice things for people and want others to like us, so we avoid being confrontational. We become experts at wrapping up emotion-laden issues in tight little packages and keeping them hidden so we don't have to deal with them. But those packages aren't like gifts with something wonderful inside. They are more similar to bombs, silently ticking away until they explode.

One example of conflict avoidance, and a symptom of Hiding Out, is not dealing with irate customers. No matter how excellent our processes are and how outstanding our crew is, there will always be irate customers. Maybe our crew had a bad day. Maybe there was an equipment failure. Or maybe everything went perfectly, but the customer is one of those impossible-to-please types. Give them a brick of gold and they will complain how heavy it is.

Whatever the reason, they aren't happy. Rather than deal with it, we ignore it. If we find ourselves avoiding callbacks to cranky customers, if we delay our response in the fervent hope that they won't call again, if the red message-waiting light on our phone blinks for days at a time, we are hiding out.

These issues may be out of sight, but they aren't out of mind. They eat away at our insides, adding to the stress every business owner already carries around on a daily basis. Tick-tick-tick. And while these hidden-away issues continue to weigh on us, they often get worse. Like a small fire that could have been extinguished with a glass of water but instead grew into a blaze, these unaddressed issues grow into major problems. In most cases, it would have been far better to defuse the issues when they were small and simple.

Accepting Mediocrity

Owners who are hiding out are very likely to accept mediocrity in employee performance. We hesitate to call employees out when their performance is substandard. We choose not to address it, telling ourselves, "I'm just nice," as if we need to choose between being nice to people and doing what's best for the company and the employee. It's obvious that addressing employee performance issues is critical to the health of a company. It may be less obvious that it's also important to the employee and that the two outcomes are tightly connected.

Most employees want to do a good job. Whether due to lack of skills, knowledge, direction, or motivation, they don't always succeed. Addressing the performance shortfall with them often will be uncomfortable. But in the long run, if they are helped to improve their performance they will feel better about themselves, about us, and about the company. And it will definitely make them more capable contributors in the future.

Closed Door

Another obvious symptom is a closed door. Every owner and manager needs some quiet time. I encourage people to set aside time every day when their door is closed to really focus on important activities without interruption. But if the default position for our door is closed, that's not a healthy sign. It tells people we don't want to be bothered, and that's not a healthy message to send. It's a sign we're hiding out.

Majoring in Minor Things / Defaulting to the Familiar

Hiding Out owners will do what's called "majoring in minor things." Rather than making tough decisions or addressing uncomfortable issues, we opt to wrap ourselves up in the secure feeling of being busy. We busy ourselves with mundane tasks that bring little value to our company or our customers. We do things that could easily, and should definitely, be done by someone else. Instead of driving the car, we're tuning the radio.

We default to familiar activities. In most cases we started out as a doer. We delivered the service to our customers. As our company and our responsibilities grew, we had to take on tasks we were either ill-prepared to perform or were just not comfortable doing. In organizations of every size, people move from doers to managers not because they displayed management skills, but because they were such good doers. This is a poor criterion for promotion. A classic example is sales. The top salesperson is often promoted to sales manager, despite the fact that selling and managing a sales team are very different roles that require entirely different skills.

For the entrepreneur who successfully grows their business, this problem is even greater. We find ourselves responsible for all manner of tasks that we have no idea how to do. What do we know about hiring and human resources? How are we supposed to know about risk management and insurance? Why didn't someone tell us we had to know something about marketing and advertising?

Rather than developing at least a baseline competency for ourselves in these areas, we hide out. We opt to perform jobs or engage in activities with which we're more familiar and comfortable. Sometimes this even includes duplicating work we've hired and are paying someone else to do. But it lets us hide out from the newer responsibilities we're trying to avoid.

Analysis Paralysis

An additional symptom of Hiding Out is developing a case of analysis paralysis. Don't confuse this with data gathering and performing due diligence prior to making a decision. Those are both valuable and productive activities, as long as they are focused on questions that warrant investigation and analysis, and as long as they result in a decision.

Analysis paralysis involves endlessly obsessing over inconsequential issues that should be resolved with only brief consideration. It also involves excessive data gathering and analysis to the extent that it stops contributing to the quality of the decision and, instead, is just a way to delay making one.

How much data do we need, and how long should we ponder on it before taking action? It varies with every company, situation, and owner. In all situations, though, it shouldn't be that hard to realize when more data or deliberation isn't appreciably improving the quality of the outcome.

Hiding Out is an exception from the other Entrepreneurial Conspiracy behaviors in one important aspect: there is no upside to it. The other behaviors can, at certain points of a company's evolution and in certain situations, actually be positives. Not so with Hiding Out.

Causes

Understanding some of the underlying causes that lead us to hide out from important information or avoid tough conversations is a first step in overcoming this tendency. What are the forces that can drive us into hiding out? Some of them run deep and can be difficult to identify or to accept. I'll get to those. But let's start with one of the easiest to see and probably one of the most important to address.

Confrontation Avoidance

Many business owners are equally unprepared or unwilling to deal with conflict. Several years ago, we surveyed our clients and learned something surprising: most of them prefer to avoid confrontation. Maybe this shouldn't have surprised me. After all, who likes confronting others and dealing with conflict? Not many people. Perhaps I was surprised because I had assumed that entrepreneurs are cut from a stronger bolt of cloth. It takes courage, intelligence, and chutzpah[21] to launch and run a business. But despite the bravery it takes to be an entrepreneur, when it comes to confronting underperforming employees or calming an angry customer, it appears that most of us get cold feet. We may tell ourselves that we're trying to protect the other person's feelings, but the truth often is that we're just as concerned about protecting our own feelings.

For many small business owners, our first employee was a family member: a parent, sibling, relative. This makes sense because we trust family members to work hard and not cheat us. We're also comfortable with the personal interaction styles we have with them since we've developed them over our lifetime. This usually works well and avoids a lot of conflict in the early stages of our business.

But as our company grows, this familiarity can become a major source of stress and cause us to hide out from having important conversations and making important decisions for our growing company.

We can try to create separation between our personal relationships and our business relationships and some people succeed at doing so. But most of us fall short in this area and we end up with blurred and confusing boundaries, hurt feelings, and poor business performance.

Fear of the Unknown and the Known

I've often commented that, as companies grow, owners and managers constantly face challenges we've never had to face before. This can be scary. The financial, competitive, and employment complexities of larger companies are very different and considerably more challenging than the ones we faced when our company was smaller.

Even for owners with advanced degrees in business, the challenges faced when the bullets start flying in the real world are different than the ones studied in the classroom. Striving to get an A on that business term paper may have put us in a cold sweat, but in hindsight it was small potatoes compared to making payroll or having to fire someone.

These challenges can be intimidating; sometimes intimidating enough to cause leaders to hide out by doing nothing or by retreating to the comfort and security of our smaller business. Even conversations we have with ourself can become debilitating: what if I confront my employee and he quits? What if I check my income statement and see we're losing money? What if I call my customer and she tells me she's unhappy or isn't going to pay me? Sometimes we choose to hide out and do nothing rather than face these unknowns.

Knowing what we're supposed to be measuring, doing, and deciding is one thing. Actually taking action on these things is another. Sometimes we're fully aware of the critical need for, and expected outcomes of, the business decisions we're about to make. Still, we deliberately choose to hide out from making them. While choosing not to make a decision is actually a decision in itself, hiding out from a decision and not letting anyone know what's going on is not.

Most businesses aren't started with the dream of becoming the next Microsoft. Most of us started our business to fulfill personal needs, whether it's physical comfort, financial security, emotional fulfillment, or something else. These personal needs seldom include things like performing breakeven analyses, equipment lease negotiations, or discharging an underperforming employee. But these are the skills it takes to lead a larger business and to elevate profitability.

Complications increase when we add family members into the mix. Things can become downright combustible when those family members inherit their jobs or when they're being asked to perform jobs they either don't want to do or don't feel they should have to do by virtue of the gene lottery. This elevates hiding out to a whole new level that involves both business and home life and can limit family interactions to a very short list of "safe" topics. Everyone in the company and the family remembers quite well what happened the last time mom or pop was asked the wrong question at the wrong time!

Analysis Paralysis

A common cause for analysis paralysis in a Hiding Out owner is that we lack the data to make an informed decision. Once we've turned a blind eye to the financials and KPIs, we don't have valid information to work with. In situations where members of the team have different opinions about the right decision, the problem is compounded. The owner who is hiding out doesn't want to create any conflict by choosing one employee's option over the other.

Based on my experience with clients, there are two other causes for Hiding Out, both related to the personality of some entrepreneurs and owners. Some are perfectionists, unwilling to accept anything less than the perfect solution or decision. Others are over-controllers who are compelled to keep a vise-tight hold on the knobs of their business. Both of these personalities drive the owner to delay action until they have 100% of the data and the perfect solution. The outcome of that drive is paralysis.

The fondest hope of the Hiding Out owner is that if we just keep pondering the issue, everyone will eventually forget that the issue ever existed and no decision will ever have to be made. Of course, that's not how the situation typically plays out.

Fatigue

A final factor that leads owners to hiding out is fatigue. "Fatigue makes cowards of us all," as Vince Lombardi liked to say. Long hours and infrequent breaks can wear down even the most energetic business owners. Many of us were younger when we started our business. Our energy was nearly boundless and working 12-hour days was the norm. But that's a pace most of us can't maintain without some serious physical and mental health issues occurring. Running a business can be exhausting and that exhaustion encourages us to turn to hiding out as a coping mechanism.

A reason for hiding out that's even greater than physical fatigue is mental and emotional exhaustion. When we're the owner of a business, all the decisions within our company ultimately come back to us. We may have delegated roles and responsibilities, but we are still the head honcho[22] who ultimately is responsible for the success—or failure—of the enterprise.

As a business grows and we find ourself in unfamiliar territory, it's easy for us to question our competence and fret ourselves into a tizzy. Similarly, when a business struggles for survival for an extended period of time, the mental fatigue can be overwhelming.

Understanding some of the underlying causes that can lead us to hiding out from important information or tough conversations is a first step in overcoming this behavior. Next is learning to recognize the consequences it can lead to in our company. Awareness of those consequences might be frightening enough to encourage us to address the tough issues we're trying to avoid by hiding out.

Consequences

Ignoring Financial Data

Imagine two travelers in a cross-country competition to see who can drive from New York City to Redondo Beach, California[23] in the shortest amount of time and using the least amount of fuel. One driver is equipped with a good sketch of the best route to take, while the other has an app on their phone that gives turn-by-turn directions, warns of law enforcement ahead, and provides ongoing feedback about detours and accidents with alternate routes to avoid them. Who are you going to put your money on?

This is a very close analogy to someone who ignores or only glances at their financials compared to the owner who digs into the details. In both cases, the owners are literally putting their money on the line. And, again, who would you put your wager on? The consequences of hiding out from our financial data, and the related responsibilities to monitor and manage financial performance, are direct and dire. To turn a common saying on its head, "Success is not an option!"

There's an interesting four-box matrix that people can be divided into regarding any skill or area of knowledge, including the ability to understand and act on financial data. This matrix is often used when assessing the appropriate training approach for learners.

In the first box of the matrix are people who are unconsciously incompetent. They don't know something, but they don't know that they don't know it. Next there are the consciously incompetent who know what they don't know. Then there are the unconsciously competent people who know something and don't realize it or just assume that everyone else knows it as well. Finally, there's the consciously competent people who know something and know they know it.

Owners who fail to take heed of their financial data could fall into either of the two incompetent categories. The unconsciously incompetent owners don't pay attention to their financials and don't realize how dangerous that is for their business. The consciously incompetent owner knows they should be paying attention but opts not to. It's excusable, but probably organizationally fatal, not to know how vital it is to follow your financials. It's another thing altogether to be aware of them yet hide out from doing so. That is shooting yourself in the financial foot.

In both cases, the outcome will be the same: a business that perpetually underperforms, fails to thrive, and is most likely doomed. There's more hope for the unconsciously incompetent owner to steer away from this course. Once enlightened about the critical importance of financial awareness, they are more likely to embrace the need for it and take appropriate action where necessary. The consciously incompetent owner, on the other hand, well understands the importance and still opts for ignorance and inaction.

Ignoring Other Performance Data

There is considerable overlap between financial data and a business's KPIs. Many small business KPIs are displayed in the financials or directly derived from them. Sales, profit, and revenue growth come straight from our financial reports. These are typically the top-line metrics of our business performance. But there are dozens of other non-financial KPIs that contribute to these top-line metrics and to the success of our company.

How long does it take us to get paid for a job (Turn on Accounts Receivable)? What is the total number of hours worked per production employee (Average Hourly Week)? How long does it take to complete projects (Average Production Time/Job)? These and other KPIs are the vital signs of our organization. Focusing on achieving strong performance on these KPIs increases the probability of company growth and profitability. Hiding out from the KPIs ignores a treasure trove of actionable information that could help us better manage our business.

By hiding out and not measuring performance, we nicely sidestep the unpleasant task of identifying and correcting areas where our business isn't delivering the desired results. Of course, simply avoiding something doesn't make it disappear. If you don't believe that, just ignore the leaking toilet in the bathroom above your kitchen. At some point, that little drip will create some huge problems. Why is the toilet on the kitchen counter?!

However, tracking financials and KPIs infers we're planning to use the information we get to take corrective action. This means holding people accountable, which in turn means we may need to have some tough conversations with some of our people. And this brings us to the next consequence.

Failure to Deal with Conflict

Hiding out from conflict creates an entirely different, but potentially just as danger-ous, set of problems related to failing to deal with conflict. Conflict exists in every organization. In many cases, that's a positive thing. As one example, there could be conflict between two ideas about how best to grow the business. An open, positive discussion of those options should result in the optimum choice. Failure to properly manage this conflict will result in missing the opportunity to do what's best for the business and possibly hard feelings on the part of the people who had opinions on the issue.

There are also the less-positive types of conflict; typically the interpersonal battles over anything from not returning items to their proper place, to personal hygiene issues, to who gets to pick their vacation days first. Failure to properly manage this conflict can leave hurt feelings, low morale, and damaged team spirit.

Dealing with conflict is hard. It generally requires a delicate approach and skills in handling difficult interpersonal situations. Owners who lack those skills often choose to simply ignore the conflict in the hope it will work itself out. In some cases, it does. The parties involved in the conflict address it and reach a solution. In other cases, the outcome is less desirable. The unaddressed conflict goes underground. Open, visible signs of the conflict disappear, but the employees involved internalize the frustration and anger. Eventually, assuming no other conflicts occur to stir up those hidden emotions, the conflict may, in fact, dissipate.

But these unresolved conflicts can also fester and grow until they erupt. Like cancer, these conflicts metastasize, growing in place and sometimes spreading throughout the organization without our knowledge. We have no idea there's a problem until these latent conflicts resurface, but now they're bigger, angrier, and far more difficult to resolve than if they would have been addressed earlier.

Fear of the Unknown and the Known

Hiding out from the actions and decisions necessary to run a successful business has obvious consequences. Our team relies on us as the leader. We are at the wheel, and they count on us to keep the company not only on track but ahead of the pack. While self-driving vehicles are on the road today, self-driving businesses don't exist. When we take our hands off the wheel of our business, it may continue moving straight ahead for some time. But as soon as an issue comes up that requires our attention or a decision, our business will be off course and headed for a ditch.

In the best-managed companies, the owner has remarkably little to do on a day-to-day basis. These organizations are staffed with capable, engaged, and empowered people guided by well-designed and implemented processes and procedures. Active owner interaction isn't required to keep the business chugging along.

Most small businesses fall short of that ideal, though. There are operational or administrative activities that are the sole purview of the owner, and if they aren't on the job and performing those activities, operations are badly hobbled. In these organizations, owners hiding out from their responsibilities result in reduced organizational momentum at best and unmitigated business disasters at worst.

Analysis Paralysis

Regarding decision making, the consequences of analysis paralysis are fairly easy to see. Important decisions go undecided. Opportunities escape. Options evaporate. And, of course, the business suffers.

One of the most cutting adjectives that can be applied to a leader is that we are indecisive. In fact, it's an oxymoron to call someone an indecisive leader. Leadership, by definition, requires making decisions. An owner who fails on that count will be held in low esteem by our employees. We would garner more respect and loyalty from our team by making bad decisions in good faith rather than making no decisions at all.

Fatigue

The pressure and stress of owning and operating a business can have a corrosive effect on humans. It can lead to near exhaustion that physically and mentally weakens us. Stress literally eats away at us, with the damage building up over time, eventually manifesting itself in some physical or mental way.

Some people blow their top. It's not pleasant to be on the receiving end of those kinds of outbursts, but they are probably therapeutic for the person angrily expressing their emotions, much like a pressure-release valve being vented.

Yet, it's not at all surprising that many of us prefer hiding out to dealing with all the stressors that come with owning and operating a business. It's common to question ourself about the number of hours we work, the family sacrifices our business demands, and the physical and emotional toll our business takes. This usually happens when we're struggling through a tough time in our business, when we're exhausted, or as we get older.

While hiding out will shield us from stress in the short term, that's not a long-term solution. And while we're hiding, the things we're hiding from continue to pile up and create a growing cascade of compounding issues.

Solutions

Ignoring Financial Data

I will instantly and proudly admit that I love looking at business financials. I can talk to owners all day about their business and listen to them tell me what they think is going well and where they need help. They often paint an overly rosy picture, either out of embarrassment at their poor performance or simply pride in the business. But when I want the truth about the health of the company, I ask them for their Profit & Loss Statement, Balance Sheet, and Cashflow Report.

It is impossible to overstate not just the value, but the absolute necessity for us to thoroughly understand the financial performance of our company. The first step in facing our financials, rather than hiding out from them, is to accept this fact. Rather than seeing financial data as volumes of impenetrable, encrypted information, it needs to be seen as a collection of stories about the decisions and actions that have taken place in the business. The important thing for a business owner is to understand the stories behind the numbers.

For those who accept the value of the financials but lack the acumen to understand and apply the information they offer, it's time to seek help. Fortunately, that help is plentiful. We almost certainly have an accountant who provides us with our financial reports and prepares our taxes. Every good accountant should be able to point us to the numbers that deserve our attention. They could be bright spots, areas of our business performance that are particularly strong, or dark spots where we're spending too much or not making as much as we should. Either way, we will be aware of them.

There may be someone in our organization who is good with financial analysis. We can tap them to help us understand what information is lurking in our credits and debits. They will no doubt feel honored that we are turning to them for help and pleased to employ their financial analysis skills. It's unlikely they will think less of us for asking. Instead, they will certainly understand that we, like many people, often struggle to decode financial data.

No matter who we rely on for help, we shouldn't let them just give us the answers to our financial questions. We shouldn't accept having them simply point to the numbers we should be looking at. We need to find out what the numbers mean; to probe, inquire, and ask what's behind the number. Where did it come from? What other numbers affect it? What numbers are affected by it? In this way, we will slowly build our financial smarts. We aren't likely to make a career change to become a CPA, but we will build self-sufficiency and competence when it comes to assessing the financial health of our business.

If we don't have someone to turn to or aren't comfortable asking for help, we should take a class. If there's a local community college or a university that offers continuing education, there's a good chance they have a course on financials for non-financial managers. There are also free, online college courses through what are called massive online open courses. These are regular college classes with instructors, homework, and classmates that are delivered online. Or by doing an online search for "finance for non-financial managers course," we should find a long list of resources to choose from.

Ignoring Other Metrics

The top financial metrics are pretty easy to identify because almost all businesses focus primarily on the same few, key measures. Since they are so widely used, we can easily find resources to help us figure out how to better understand and address them. That's a great start, but owners who are hiding out need to work harder, and scratch a bit deeper, to identify the metrics that are unique to service businesses and specifically to our business.

There are so many aspects to managing a business that can't be found in a single, holy grail KPI that provides all the needed information. It will require identifying multiple KPIs. The search for the right or best ones to use begins by figuring out what our targets are, what aspects of our business have the greatest potential for additional growth, and which are the deepest low spots of our performance.

Dealing with Conflict

If you've committed to stop hiding out (good for you!), this means you now will need to face the sometimes-unpleasant task of addressing conflicts. This could include beefs between employees. Or disputes between you and an employee, supplier, or others you and your business interact with. Aside from the organizational benefits of reduced conflict, there's also a very personal benefit. We need to get over the concerns about the potential pitfalls and see the bigger picture. As an owner, in most cases we are aware of the conflict and are concerned about it. It weighs on us as we constantly recalculate the cost/benefit of getting involved. This adds stress to our day.

Resolving conflict will not only relieve us of the concern and worry we're no doubt feeling, but it will also help the other parties to be better people and employees. It may help them improve in areas they may not realize need improvement.

Regardless of who is involved and the nature of the conflict, there are four options for resolution: Avoid, Accommodate, Compete, or Collaborate.

When we avoid a conflict, we stand by and let the people involved work it out on their own. This is the right choice for trivial disagreements. Still, we need to take a watchful-waiting approach to be sure it doesn't escalate. Small conflicts can sometimes turn into something very large and destructive. Wildfires that started with one spark or a single match can grow and destroy thousands of acres of woods. For conflicts related to matters of importance or over trivial issues that have escalated to a major brouhaha, it's our responsibility to get involved.

The next option is to accommodate—basically letting the other person have their way. This is a good choice when we are more concerned about maintaining a good relationship than we are with "winning" the conflict. There's nothing wrong with this option, especially for trivial matters. But we need to be careful about accommodating too often or we will be revealed as someone who prefers to avoid conflict and can be intimidated. If employees, suppliers, and others know we're always eager to accommodate, they may take advantage of that weakness.

The third conflict resolution option is to compete, which emphasizes accomplishing a task or winning over maintaining relationships. It is the speediest option because we simply dictate the outcome. That's okay if it's done for the right reasons. For instance, if the issue is urgent and there's no time for the other options. Or if it's a critical issue and we are absolutely confident in the correctness of one side. But people also choose to compete mainly because they want to "win," which is usually a bad reason. It is sometimes necessary to remind people who's in charge, but keep in mind that choosing to compete too often breeds anger, frustration, and resentment among others.

The final conflict-resolution option is to collaborate, which has the greatest potential for long-term success in most situations. When we collaborate in resolving conflict, we maintain strong relationships while still accomplishing the task. This approach typically results in the best outcome for us and our company. But this can also be the most difficult option to use successfully and is usually the most time consuming. It often requires negotiation skills and a willingness on both sides to give a little.

We won't exclusively use any of the four options for resolving conflict. In each situation we need to weigh the variables and choose what seems to be the appropriate option under the circumstances.

Analysis Paralysis

Overcoming analysis paralysis is often easier when we segment the decision making into smaller chunks or steps. For most decision making, the basic and proven process includes five steps.

We start by first defining and framing the decision, being very clear on what it is we need to decide. It's valuable to write the required decision down, as capturing it in words has a way of ensuring clarity.

Second, we gather and analyze the data. With actual data to consider and evaluate, the correct or optimal choice becomes much easier to identify. It may be useful to divide the big decision into smaller ones. For example, trying to decide between expanding our current location or moving to a new, larger facility would involve analyzing and making decisions about factors like the cost, business disruption, quality of the new versus current space, etc.

With data gathering and analysis complete, the third step is to evaluate the options and make a choice. If we took the mathematical route, the decision is made based on the score. We shouldn't be surprised if, once we see the results, we find ourself going back and adjusting the data. Sometimes it's apparent that our math didn't correctly rank the options. Just as often, though, it's because we didn't get the answer we wanted, so we go looking for ways to tweak the data to give us that answer. This may be okay. The evaluation process will no doubt have clarified issues in our mind that were hazy before. But if others were involved in the process and we arbitrarily ignore the outcome and make a decision contrary to what the process indicated, we shouldn't expect much support from them when it comes to implementing the outcome. It's likely they also won't be eager to participate in our next decision-making activity.

With our decision made, the fourth step is to implement it. Thanks to the rigor we applied, there's a high probability it will be a good decision and deliver the benefits we envisioned. Of course, most decisions include variables that are out of our control or there are unintended consequences of the decision. That's why there's a fifth step—audit the results. If things don't turn out as expected, then we need to go back to step three and reevaluate our options to see if there's another possibility that will deliver better results.

Fatigue

The best solution for addressing fatigue depends on where a business is in its life cycle. If the business is still very young and we are in the go-go startup stage, then we should probably resign ourself to exhaustion for a while. There's no getting around the fact that it takes a tremendous amount of work, most of it by the owner, to establish a new business. If we find ourself hiding out at this point and unable to bear up under the pressure, we should probably rethink our career choice. It may be that small business ownership is just not for us.

If our business is well established and fatigue is still an issue, the prospects for a solution are much better. We have, or at least we had, the energy and stamina to launch and manage a small business. But that smaller business presented a less-taxing situation than managing a larger business. The scope and range of required management skills is vastly different and far more intimidating.

Rather than hiding out, we should share the load by engaging our employees to a greater extent in managing and operating the business. Doing so will take a huge load off our shoulders. Naturally, we can't just hand out our responsibilities willynilly. It needs to be done thoughtfully and carefully. This requires delegation skills which, again, can be strengthened using the training resources discussed earlier. This is also a skill we will need to continue as our business grows.

As a young child, when our troubles closed in on us and we felt overwhelmed, we probably took refuge in bed. We pulled the covers up over our head and the world outside vanished. Even today, as adults, the idea is probably appealing sometimes. Just make it all go away. But even as a child, we knew we couldn't hide out for long. Sooner or later, mom or dad would come up and compel us to get out of bed and deal with whatever it was we were hiding from.

As a business owner or manager, hiding out may provide a similar, short-term respite. What it doesn't provide is leadership or confidence in our abilities. While we are hiding out, our business slows, stumbles, and goes off course. The longer we hide out, the worse the problem becomes.

In the meantime, our employees will be frustrated by our failure to fulfill our responsibilities and concerned about our weakness in confronting problems and addressing issues. It's tough to have confidence in and feel a commitment to someone who shirks what is clearly their responsibility as the owner or leader of the company.

And hiding out also compounds three of the previous four behaviors we've discussed. While hiding out, we increase the chance of Blurred Vision because we aren't focusing on the metrics that are essential to business success. When we are hiding out, we aggravate the No Accountability behavior. We aren't fully engaged with the business, which means we can't be held accountable for our failure to perform. And hiding out may lead to E-Drift. A great way to take our mind off those business worries that encouraged the hiding out is to shop for a new toy, right?. Hmmm, how big of a motor can I fit on my boat?

In the next chapter, I'll describe the last of the behaviors that comprise the Entrepreneurial Conspiracy. Instead of Hiding Out, where the owner becomes a shadowy, out-of-sight, player in business operations, we'll explore the psyche of owners who put themselves front and center.

CHAPTER 7
SWOLLEN EGO

When we are in a leadership position, and especially when we are the owner, it's easy to be seduced by the power and authority we possess and the deference others show to us. We are the boss, the big kahuna, top dog, numero uno. But giving in to the allure of being at the top of our organizational heap can set the stage for our own demise.

A Swollen Ego convinces us that the rules of business and social decorum apply to everyone else but not to us. It keeps us from asking questions that would allow us to make better decisions or to question our assumptions. It tempts us to take unnecessary risks and make knee-jerk decisions for all the wrong reasons.

In his book, *How the Mighty Fall*, business guru and author Jim Collins outlines five distinct stages that companies go through as they slip into decline. The very first stage is "Hubris born of success." In other words, the egos and arrogance of company leaders cause them to believe they're entitled to success, and that the rules of business no longer apply to them. They mistakenly think they're insulated from the risk of failure. While Collins writes about billion-dollar, multinational enterprises, I've witnessed the same principle play itself out in small businesses. When the owner's ego is out of control, it's never a matter of if the company will stumble and decline. It's only a matter of when. While the Bible isn't often looked to as a source of business advice, in this case it offers this wisdom: "Pride goeth before destruction, and a haughty spirit before a fall."

In a roundabout manner, Chris Zook and James Allen also write about the impact hubris, ego, and arrogance can have on business in their book *The Founder's Mentality*. The results of a survey they conducted showed, "A remarkable 94 percent of barriers [to profitable growth] cited by large-company executives had their roots in internal dysfunction and lack of internal capabilities." It's no different with small business executives, and while all the internal dysfunction in our company might not be centered on ego issues—specifically our issues as the owner—much of it is.

One of the major character flaws I see in business owners is that we tend to have a very high opinion of ourself. A healthy ego isn't a bad thing. It is a feeling of self-worth that provides a foundation for taking the risks that are inherent in starting and building a business. Our self-confidence could be seen as an extension of our ego. We need to believe in ourself or no one else will. The problem occurs when self-worth morphs into a feeling of self-importance and our ego begins to swell and manifest itself in unhealthy ways. Confidence becomes arrogance, and while confidence is a much-admired trait, arrogance seldom is. If you doubt that, just finish this sentence: "He is an arrogant _____." I would bet the noun you use isn't complimentary!

Harold Geneen, the American businessman most famous for serving as president of the ITT Corporation, said, "The worst disease which can afflict business executives in their work is not, as popularly supposed, alcoholism[24]; it's egotism."

Symptoms

Swollen Ego can be particularly difficult for us to identify in ourself because it masks itself. People afflicted with Swollen Ego are blinded to its effect. Like so many unproductive or unhealthy behaviors, it's easy for us to notice in others what we fail to see in ourself. That's the nature of this behavior. But the symptoms are there to those of us who can clear our vision long enough to see them. In owners with a swollen ego, self-awareness typically doesn't exist.

In his book *What Got You Here Won't Get You There*, author and executive coaching expert Marshall Goldsmith suggests using a simple test to assess how well we are managing our ego. See how easy it is for us to say "Please," "Thank you," and "I'm sorry."

Many business owners struggle with saying these three basic phrases with sincerity. Too many owners feel that their position excuses them from having to ask permission, show gratitude, or apologize. Nothing could be further from the truth. I have found that the easier it is to say these phrases, the better managed a person's ego is.

A more relevant and accurate measure of Swollen Ego is considering how often employees and suppliers confront us. In a healthy organization, when someone sees danger approaching, they will alert the boss. If an employee makes a mistake that is likely to have some fallout in the future, they will give management a heads-up to give them a chance to prepare a response or take proactive, corrective action. If an employee perceives some defect in our business strategy that they think can be corrected, they will raise the idea with their superiors. In a healthy organization, employees feel empowered to be constantly alert for ways to enhance processes and bring their ideas to the leadership. Suppliers, also, will be eager to present alternate products or services that may provide a competitive or cost advantage.

We won't see those kinds of valuable ideas and suggestions being brought forward in an organization led by someone with a swollen ego. A swollen ego seems to have a debilitating effect on an owner's hearing ability. They have no interest in listening to input from others, because they think they already have all the answers. As a result, employees may be afraid to bring forward information that's contrary to what the owner wants or believes. Even worse, employees may relish seeing their egotistical owner get a smackdown.

Some time ago, I was working with a client whose swollen ego paid a visit every time he felt challenged by an employee. To explain his reasoning for not taking employees' suggestions, he would say, "Because I'm the O-W-N-E-R." While this might have made him feel important, it did little to build an empowered workplace. His people soon learned to stop offering suggestions.

People who work for or with someone with a swollen ego are afraid to speak truth to their emperor. They learn that the owner is overly confident in themself and their actions, and therefore typically ignores the input and contributions of others. You only have to shoot people down once or twice to effectively shut off the flow of new ideas and useful information they have to offer.

Our Need to be Right

Some years ago, I was having a discussion with my then-17-year-old son about a class he was taking in school. Before I knew it, the conversation shifted from the original discussion about the content of the class to which one of us was right about the content. This incident made me think about how often the same thing happens in business. As business owners, we're called upon to make a lot of decisions. The more decisions we make correctly, the more likely we are to be successful. But it's easy to trip ourselves up when we become more interested in being right than in making the right decision.

In his book *Mind Set!*, author John Naisbitt writes about the limiting effect our need to be right can have on us. "People are culturally conditioned to have to be right. The parents are right, the teacher is right, the boss is right. Who is right overrules what is right. Couples have huge quarrels about considerations that are forgotten as the struggle for who is right rages on. Having to be right becomes a barrier to learning and understanding. It keeps you away from growing, for there is no growth without changing, correcting, and questioning yourself."

The need to be right means we sometimes stop asking for or listening to the advice of people in our organization, because it just takes too much energy to change our opinion and admit someone else might be right. When this happens, it becomes a self-limiting exercise.

Feeling Entitled

Beyond the failure to listen, owners with Swollen Ego display a general contempt for their employees and others "below them." Their sense of entitlement grows stronger with each business success. Based on what they've accomplished and who they are, these owners feel they are owed something from others and from the world. They expect to have the best seat at the table, to be served first, and get the best cut of whatever is being served.

Do people increase their status and wealth by being selfish and self-centered, or do people become more selfish as their status increases? This question may have been answered by an experiment where the researcher manipulated people's feelings of social class. Some of the results were reported in *Scientific American* magazine in an article titled "How Wealth Reduces Compassion."

> The researchers asked participants to spend a few minutes comparing themselves either to people better off or worse off than themselves financially. Afterwards, participants were shown a jar of candy and told that they could take home as much as they wanted. They were also told that the leftover candy would be given to children in a nearby laboratory. Those participants who had spent time thinking about how much better off they were compared to others ended up taking significantly more candy for themselves—leaving less behind for the children.[25]

....

It would seem that people with a grander feeling about themselves tend to be more selfish and less compassionate. Many other studies bear out this fact, but there can be perhaps no simpler evidence than the case of the stolen bagels.

In their book *Freakanomics*, authors Steven D. Levitt and Stephen J. Dubner tell the tale of an executive who got into the habit of bringing bagels each time his department won a contract. It then morphed to an every-Friday habit that eventually grew to him bringing in 15 dozen bagels a week. One day, his company came under new management that didn't suit the bagel-bringing executive. He decided to do something different, so he quit his job and started selling bagels!

He did it on an honor system. Each morning, he delivered bagels and left a cash basket at each stop on his route, which consisted of professional and office buildings. Each afternoon, he would pick up the cash and the leftovers. His venture was very successful, growing to 140 stops each day and 8,400 bagels a week. His honor system provided an interesting window into the honesty of people, because he knew, on a percentage basis, how many bagels were not paid for. One of his most striking observations related to a company housed in a three-story building. As is often the case, the top floor was reserved for executives, while the sales, service, and administrative people were on the lower two floors. The executives on the top floor consistently paid for their bagels less often than those below them, floor-wise and status-wise.

Checking Out

While a sense of entitlement and superiority are the hallmarks of a swollen ego, there is also one more significant symptom. It's "going Hollywood," referring to our pursuit of the trappings of success rather than success itself. We become so pleased with ourself and our success that we check out from our business a bit. Rather than remain engaged, we allow our attention to be diverted to other activities and things.

Regarding the acquisition of new things—the fancy car, boat, vacation home, or other tangible sign of our status—this appears to be very similar to the behavior of someone in E-Drift. The motivation for E-Drift, however, differs. In that case, the bright shiny things are acquired primarily as a reward for the owner's hard work. With Swollen Ego, that may also be the case, but more important is that the things demonstrate to the world what a successful and powerful person the owner is. Either way, those luxury items are a distraction from the business and can become a source of resentment to those who work for and with us, and possibly to our customers and suppliers as well.

Regarding walling ourself off from close contact with our business, a conversation I had with the owner of a $1.5M company illustrates the potential problems. The owner had checked out of his company several years prior and was spending his time dabbling in non-business-related activities. He voiced concern to me that the company he built and the lifestyle he was enjoying were being threatened. His long-time office manager/bookkeeper, the trusted person who had kept the company running, abruptly left, and several new competitors had entered his market. He was faced with having to re-engage with his company to try to regain the momentum needed to overcome the competitive challenges of the two newcomers. He learned that when we check out of our company, we compromise our motivation to make the hard decisions and confront the tough issues needed to run a successful business.

There's a world of difference between being physically absent and mentally checking out. In a large organization or one with multiple locations there's no way the CEO can be physically present everywhere every day. This doesn't mean they can't be actively engaged with the business, thanks to a variety of technology. Even if they're not there physically, they can make their presence felt and remain fully mentally engaged in the company. But when an owner checks out mentally, it doesn't matter where their body is. Whether they're in the office or elsewhere, their mind isn't on the business.

Causes

The seeds of Swollen Ego exist in every entrepreneur. Businesses aren't built by people with small egos. It requires confidence, courage, and assertiveness. In other words, it requires a big, healthy, strong ego. We need to accept the fact that being an entrepreneur places us in a high-risk category for having a swollen ego.

Confidence and Success

Many businesses were started and built by owners because of very personal reasons. We wanted to live up to our parents' and teachers' expectations, or maybe to disprove the low expectations they had. We felt the need to show complete strangers how wrong they were in their assessments of us. Maybe we yearned for the admiration and accolades of our friends or community members. These wants and needs are all causes or symptoms of an ego that is hungry for expression. The problem is that the more successful we become, the more our ego competes with us for continued success. The stakes for winning and losing continue to escalate and, unfortunately, so does our ego. We'll never escape it. We can only hope to control it.

Self-Esteem

There is an interesting dichotomy in that a swollen ego can result from both very low and very high self-esteem. The ego that grows from very high self-esteem is fairly obvious because the two are so closely related. Having favorable or positive self-esteem is very healthy, but when self-esteem becomes over-inflated, it turns into a swollen ego.

The role of low self-esteem is less obvious but probably just as common. We probably all know someone who is always eager to share examples of how wonderful they are, but in reality, has little to back up those claims. They puff themselves up to others to compensate for their lack of skills and knowledge or feelings of inadequacy. They are, in the cowboy vernacular, all hat and no cattle. Well-known business expert John Kotter said that, "Ego is the anesthetic that dulls the pain of ignorance."

How does someone go from having a healthy ego to one that becomes dangerously swollen? It starts out innocently enough. We launch our business and make some good decisions that lead to success. We make some money. We get a title (or we give ourselves one). We start having employees who turn to us for direction. We have suppliers who are eager to do business with us. People around town meet us and say, "Oh, you own such-and-such business, right?!" All of these events are great. They are a sign of a growing business. But they also feed our ego like an all-you-can-eat buffet. We start to tell ourself, "Wow, I really am something. I am successful, important, and known around the community. I am awesome!"

It's all so wonderful and makes us feel good about ourselves. But, if we're not careful to keep our ego in check, the swelling starts.

Ironically, as our business and our success grow, it becomes increasingly important for us to manage our ego. In the early days of our business, a swollen ego can help us bull our way through the hardships. "I am" (we tell ourselves) "unstoppable, unbeatable, and tireless!" Our healthy ego is the foundation that sustains us through those frenetic, early years. Since we are probably on our own in the beginning, there's no one for our outsized ego to harm or offend. But as we begin to add other people, our success increasingly depends on others' input and efforts, which requires us to tame our ego and share the credit and praise with our employees.

Unfortunately, a swollen ego is a bit like fat cells—very hard to get rid of. When we diet, we don't actually lose any fat cells; they shrink, but they don't disappear. There is a well-known axiom of physics that states, "Nature abhors a vacuum." This is very true with fat cells, as our body experiences the food cravings necessary to refill those cells with a fresh supply of fat. This fact of biology has derailed many a diet. We may know all too well that it's possible to lose weight but very hard to keep it off. Similarly, once an ego has been swollen and we've experienced the pleasure of standing above and apart from the crowd, it is hard to shrink it to the size of a mere mortal's ego. But shrink it we must.

Low Emotional Intelligence (EI)

One of the tenets of emotional intelligence is the ability to identify and manage our own emotions. Many experts feel that emotional intelligence is a vital part of leadership.

Research conducted by Rutgers University illustrates how important emotional intelligence is to business success. It said that emotional intelligence has double the impact of intellectual intelligence. Some people, including Daniel Goleman who wrote several books on the topic, believe it plays an even greater role. Goleman states:

> It's not that IQ and technical skills are irrelevant. They do matter, but…they are the entry-level requirements for executive positions. My research, along with other recent studies, clearly shows that emotional intelligence is the sine qua non of leadership. Without it, a person can have the best training in the world, an incisive, analytical mind, and an endless supply of smart ideas, but he still won't make a great leader.[26]

....

There are five factors of emotional intelligence, most of which relate to Swollen Ego: self-awareness; self-management; drive; empathy; ability to build relationships.

It's easy to draw a line directly from four of the five factors to Swollen Ego, with drive being the only one not included. People with a swollen ego lack self-awareness. They see theirself as floating above the crowd, superior to others in almost every way. They fail to see their emotional shortcomings … including the fact that they are suffering from Swollen Ego.

Self-management relates to using what we know about our emotions to manage them in a way that motivates us and generates positive interactions. When blinded by a swollen ego, we have little concern about the emotions, concerns, and needs of others.

Empathy, the ability to understand and share the feelings of another, is hard to come by when we are so busy telling ourself how wonderful we are.

Given the state of those three factors of emotional intelligence, it's obvious that an owner with a swollen ego will be a poor builder of positive relationships. What we build instead is usually a high level of resentment among employees and other business associates.

Aside from being a vital leadership skill, our level of emotional intelligence may actually be a good predictor of how much we will earn, according to a study published in the *Journal of Organizational Behavior*.[27] The researchers looked at a trait called "emotion recognition ability," which determines how well we can sense (and make sense of) other people's emotions from their face and voice. Researchers tested and measured it along with other interpersonal skills such as their social awareness, networking savviness, and perceived trustworthiness. High emotional recognition was linked to a higher salary, even after controlling for salary-bumping factors such as age, gender, education, work experience, and work hours. It seems that the better people are at recognizing emotions (the higher their EI), the stronger their abilities to effectively interact with others.

Some of us may only grudgingly admit our ego has swollen and poses problems for us and for our business, but most of us feel we're too busy to do anything about it. Seriously? We have time to work on marketing to acquire new customers, look for ways to make more money, and try to find hirable workers, yet we don't have time to address this huge threat to our company? Or do we just not believe it's a threat or want to address it? If we look at the consequences, we may change our mind.

Consequences

Like Hiding Out, having a Swollen Ego conceals the other four behaviors of the Entrepreneurial Conspiracy, making them harder to detect. Owners who are hiding out don't see the other behaviors because they are disengaged from the business. Owners with a swollen ego, on the other hand, may be aware of the behaviors but are unconcerned by them. These Swollen Ego owners may feel they are too important to get involved with the resulting problems, or they may believe that the behaviors will automatically be overcome by their tremendous wisdom and leadership skills. The reality is that those other behaviors act like an undiagnosed but critical disease that progresses at an increasingly rapid rate. The symptoms pile up and reinforce one another, accelerating the business's downward spiral. Eventually, the behaviors will assuredly have a serious, and possibly fatal, consequence on the business.

Going Hollywood

Lee Iacocca, former chairman of Chrysler Corporation, accomplished what many consider to be one of the greatest turnarounds in business history when he led Chrysler back from the brink of bankruptcy in 1979. As with many companies, when Chrysler was looking over the fiscal cliff at impending disaster, Iacocca and his leadership team became very focused on what needed to be done. That focus faded, though, when they succeeded in their turnaround. Business leaders, government officials, and the media heaped praise on the organization, focusing most of it on Iacocca himself. Iacocca graced the cover of *Time* magazine not once but twice, pitched margarine in a TV ad, and was even considered as a candidate for president of the United States.

Whose ego wouldn't get inflated with all the attention and accolades? Iacocca's obviously did, and he checked out. Who wants the grind of managing a business when you can spend your time hobnobbing with the rich, powerful, and famous? People remember well that it didn't take long before we were once again reading about Chrysler's financial woes. As I mentioned earlier, Dr. Dieter Zetsche, one of Iacocca's successors, would later remark, "Every time we get successful, we get stupid."

Supremely confident in our business powers, we start making decisions based on emotion and not on facts. We stop asking questions or gathering input. We don't need to ask or rely on others, we think, because our accomplishments, fancy titles, and expensive things show how wonderful we are.

It's easy to let our ego convince us that we had more to do with our success than we actually did. We dismiss the impact that sponsors, mentors, and blind luck had on our success. We forget how fortunate we are and what a privilege it is to own a business in a free country. Every accomplishment we achieve in our life and in our business is a privilege in which others played a part. These accomplishments carry with them a responsibility to the others involved. We'd do well not to let our ego blind us to this fact.

Ignoring the Ides

Perhaps no story in history better demonstrates the tragic consequences of arrogance driven by a swollen ego as that of the murder of Julius Caesar. Caesar went to the Forum on the Ides of March,[28] apparently unaware he was to die there that day. But how could he not have known? A soothsayer warned him to "beware the Ides of March." There were signs any superstitious Roman would have recognized: an owl hooting during the day and a lion running through the streets. Even Caesar's loving wife, Calpurnia, begged him to stay home. If all that wasn't enough, consider that Artemidorus, a teacher in Rome, wrote down the names of the conspirators and tried to give the note to Caesar—three times! The last time was just moments before Brutus and the boys attacked.

Caesar felt he was invincible, and he paid for his arrogance with his life. While the story of Caesar is tragic, it's not unique. The corporate landscape is littered with the names of once great business leaders whose careers were destroyed and their companies seriously compromised, because they allowed their success to turn into arrogance fueled by an inflated opinion of themselves.

The good news is that, just as with Julius Caesar, we have plenty of warning signs that our business, and the decisions we're making, are being overly influenced by a swollen ego. Unfortunately, just like with Caesar, too many times we ignore the warnings. We may go through the motions of asking people for their opinions, but everyone has learned to recognize this for what it really is—a thinly veiled attempt to have others nod their approval as they rubber-stamp the decisions already made.

Blind Confidence

Making decisions while under the influence of a swollen ego is like getting behind the wheel of a car when we're drunk. Whether under the effects of too many Seagram's and sodas or Swollen Ego, our reasoning is clouded. We easily convince ourself that we are fully functioning and ready to roll, but everyone around us knows better. We put our company and ourself at great risk when making decisions that are distorted by our ego rather than based on informed data. I refer to this as "situational blindness," where we don't see situations as they are but rather as we want them to be. We bend reality to fit our needs—in this case, the need to feed our ego. We don't do our due diligence, we fail to consider the long-term consequences of our decisions, or we simply ignore input from our advisors and employees because we think we're above all that.

Think about that Big Dog competitor who swaggers his way into every convention or networking event you attend. You know the one—the loud, larger-than-life guy everybody swoons over. The one we might secretly envy and want to be more like. But we also secretly relish the thought of someone or something taking him down a notch. An inflated ego invites the enmity of most of his employees. A few may admire that trait, but most will find it distasteful. They will root for, and work hard for, the owner who doesn't flaunt their success, but instead accepts it humbly.

So, now our company is hit with what attorneys might call double jeopardy. Not only are our business decisions being made blindly, but our best people become demotivated when they find their input is no longer valued. Rather than feeling like respected members of a vibrant team, they start to feel like voiceless cogs in a spinning wheel. And they are going to spin themselves right out the door.

Every business owner and manager spends a great deal of time worrying about our outside competitors. What we fail to realize is that some of the greatest threats to our business actually come from within our company. Swollen Ego is one of them.

We actually have very little control over our outside competitors, but we have complete control over our ego. Maybe this year the biggest competitive decision each of us should make is whether we're ready to address this internal competitor.

Solutions

The most common cure for Swollen Ego is typically painful. It comes in the form of a serious blow dealt by a competitor, customer, or employee. A competitor steals a big account, a major customer drops us for another supplier, or our best employee leaves for another company. We are faced with the stark realization that we are not quite as wonderful as we thought. These business traumas are bitter medicine that, hopefully, will encourage some introspection, leading to a realization that these wounds were self-inflicted.

Our pain and public embarrassment can be avoided by proactively bringing about change from within. This might be harder to accomplish, but it's usually much less painful and more effective in the long run. It is in line with a radical approach to checking our ego (that clearly is not for everyone) suggested by Father Richard Rohr of the Center for Action and Contemplation. He writes, "I have prayed for years for one good humiliation a day, and then, I must watch my reaction to it."

Let's try to avoid the humiliation and try introspection, instead. How do we get a grip on our ego when our ego has a grip on us? It starts by changing the way we think about our success and replacing our self-importance with humility. This can be very challenging. In fact, this could be the single-most difficult personal change suggested in this entire book. Even the most swollen ego is surprisingly fragile. But if we can retool our perspective about what made our business a success and realize there's more to it than our wonderful self, it will have an amplifying effect on our efforts to change all the other behaviors that comprise the Entrepreneurial Conspiracy.

Be Humble

Let me start by, again, acknowledging what we have all accomplished. Someone who successfully launches a business is the embodiment of the American Dream. We created something that provides not only services to our customers but a living for us, our family, our employees, and our suppliers. High five!

But no matter how hard we have worked to make our dreams a reality, a lot of our success happened at the moment we were born if our birthplace was the United States. We had the good luck to be born in a prosperous, democratic, free-market country where everyone has the opportunity to chart their own path in life. In many, perhaps most, countries, that's simply not the case. Born in another place, even the most intelligent, personable, and gifted individual might never have the opportunity to rise above the conditions and class they were born into.

We may have been born to parents who provided for us, guided us, and perhaps funded our education or the start of our business. Would we have succeeded without them?

We live in a country where we have the rule of law, so our business can't be capriciously taken away from us by the government. Would we have invested so much of ourself in the business if we lived in a country or culture where that wasn't the case?

We may be sitting in the catbird seat[29] now, but there is no end to the ways we could be pushed out of it at a moment's notice. We are all one event away from being knocked off our perch. Keeping that thought in mind may help us ratchet down the pride and feel a bit more humble. Success can be fragile and fleeting.

I talked earlier about Dale Carnegie's belief that feelings follow actions. So, what actions might we take to dial down the arrogance and ramp up the humility? Consider the phrase "carry the water." It's a Zen concept related to self-enlightenment. In practice, it refers to not putting ourself above the work that we expect others to do. It encourages us to look for ways to carry more than our fair share of the load. If we are a member of a committee or team, perhaps we could volunteer to do the job nobody else wants. To take it a step further, we could do it with a smile!

We could grab a shovel or a broom and put it to use. There's always a mess that needs cleaned up, even when it's not our own. We could remind ourself of our good fortune by volunteering at a soup kitchen, homeless shelter, or food pantry. As our success and affluence increase over time, it's easy to forget, or intentionally overlook, those less fortunate.

Revisiting Marshall Goldsmith's advice, if we are in the wrong or have made a mistake, we should own it, accept blame, and apologize. There are few things more off-putting than when someone blames others, and few things more honorable than accepting blame where it may not, in fact, be ours to take. But doing so will often earn the respect and trust of the people around us.

It doesn't have to be fancy. Just a basic "I'm sorry," or "My apologies," is sufficient, as long as it's sincere. We don't even need to offer a reason for the apology. Sometimes that's better, because explanations can sound like excuses. Apologies are appropriate when we miss a deadline, when we drop the ball, show up late, misunderstand, show impatience or anger, or just screw up. As Dale Carnegie advised, "If you are wrong, admit it quickly, emphatically."

If we are successful in developing a sense of humility—and I hope we are because it is essential to being an effective and respected leader—our eyes will likely be opened to seeing things in new and beneficial ways. We will be able to experience new revelations by answering the question posed by Ryan Holiday in his book *Ego Is the Enemy*: "What am I missing right now that a more humble person might see?"

Be Grateful

Being grateful goes hand in hand with being humble. We should start by acknowledging the fact that many of the traits we have that enabled us to be successful are traits we were born with. We deserve some credit for being such hardworking, driven, and determined leaders, but those traits were largely baked into our DNA the day our mother brought us into the world."

Even with that great start, we've all been helped along the way and we should express our thanks to the people who supported our pursuit of business success. Perhaps we should put a Post-It Note on our desk for a few weeks, reminding us to "Thank someone today." We coud do the same thing on our refrigerator at home. Expressing gratitude pays off in many ways. It builds stronger relationships with the people we thank and encourages them to continue or repeat the actions we thanked them for.

Be grateful for the small things. Many times, on cold winter days (and we have a lot of those in Northeastern Ohio), I will find myself being grateful for the fact that I have a warm home and a full stomach. You and I know the hunger that comes from missing a meal because we had to work late or attend a meeting. Few of us have experienced the hunger that comes from not being able to afford to go to the grocery store.

The opportunities for gratitude are endless. Being aware of them, and expressing them, helps keep us grounded and humble.

Be Courteous

We are, unfortunately, surrounded by rudeness in its many forms. Someone cuts in front of us in a line. They park in a place they shouldn't. They interrupt others to interject their opinion or position. They leave a mess rather than cleaning up after themself. All these forms of rudeness stem from their sense of entitlement and the thought that they are better than others. When others see this kind of behavior, they typically think less of the individual.

Don't Be That Person

The reasons people give for not being courteous are legion, but one that stands out is people feeling they're overloaded with work and have no time to be nice. Really?! Being courteous doesn't need to take extra time but it does take being mindful of opportunities. Here are a few.

Open doors. In many cases, modern technology has taken care of this for us, which might help explain why so few of us think to hold a door open for others when they don't open automatically. At the same time, it might also be why it's appreciated so much when someone does. Opening doors isn't a courtesy that only extends to grandmas. It should be extended to people of all ages and genders.

Put your phone down. Mobile technology has become such a pervasive part of our everyday life that many times we're not aware how frequently they distract our attention. We're in a conversation or in a meeting and feel compelled to acknowledge (viewing is acknowledging) the tweet, the text, or the call. Doing so sends a subtle message that "I have no idea what this is about, but it must be more important than you."

When our kids were growing up, my wife and I instituted a mobile-free zone at the dinner table. Dinner time was family time, and we didn't want it interrupted with "emergency" calls. Where were all these emergencies before the advent of mobile phones? It makes you wonder how civilization continued to advance when people actually had to wait to make a phone call. Or before phones even existed! I'm convinced that most of today's "gottas" are really just "wannas."

Say "Please." This one's pretty basic, but sometimes the most basic things are also the most important. Saying "Please" is one of them. Too often, we lose this fundamental skill as we advance in our career. Title, prestige, and elevated income can deceive us into thinking we've risen above the act of saying "Please" anymore. That's a mistake. We never outgrow the need.

Say "Thank you." This is another of those basic courtesies we may think we've outgrown as we become increasingly more important, or more accurately, self-important. But failing to thank others actually telegraphs how self-important we think we are and that's never good for business. Saying "Thank you" to a peer is a sign of respect. It lets the person know we place value on the comment they made or the effort they put forth. Saying "Thank you" to someone who reports to us sends a special message of appreciation and importance to them.

To elevate our appreciation to greater heights, we can send an email or, better yet, a written note briefly expressing our appreciation. One of our suppliers recalls that, when he worked for a big company, the president sent him a three-sentence note thanking him for his work on a project. That note remained pinned to the wall of his office for years, a daily reminder of a small form of gratitude that took the president less than a minute to write. That's quite a payoff on a simple and small act of executive courtesy. The words "Please" and "Thank you" have an amazing power to build success.

Be careful to avoid couching courtesy in sarcasm. We may think we're being funny when someone who is frequently late shows up early one day, and our response is, "Hey, look who is here before starting time for a change!" While the recipient of that comment may take it in the spirit intended, they could just as easily see it as a big slice of sarcasm, which is unlikely to encourage them to show up early again. Better to say with sincerity, "Thanks for coming in early today. I appreciate the extra effort!"

Basic courtesies in the workplace can influence how much coworkers want to collaborate with us on projects, how approachable people view us when they have problems, and even the level of stress others feel when being around us. The American Psychological Association estimates that workplace stress costs the U.S. economy $500 billion a year. That's a lot of money! And it makes a lot of sense when you consider decreases in work effort, lost workdays, and even declines in commitment to our organizations that the stress fostered by incivility and discourtesies can cause.

While I have no data to support this claim, I've got to believe that people who are courteous are more likely to win customers, advance in their career, and get along better in life than people who aren't. I am not naïve enough to believe that good guys always finish first, but I do believe they do so more often and earn the respect, trust, and loyalty of their employees when they do. It doesn't matter how trends, fashions, or ideals change over time. Courtesy is always in style and will be a powerful tool in efforts to manage Swollen Ego.

Be Considerate

We have all probably heard the advice to "care more than others think is wise." I would be willing to bet we have never heard anyone say, "He just cares too much about others" in a negative way. Whether the others are customers or employees, it is hard to care too much, and caring for others is universally seen as a sign of good character and trustworthiness.

As psychotherapist and business author Morris Shechtman points out in his book *Working Without a Net,* there's a big difference between "caring for" and "taking care of" and it's easy to confuse the two. When we take care of someone, we enable them. While this isn't always a bad thing, if we're not careful it can get in the way of a person's growth. It can take away their responsibility for making decisions and learning from their mistakes.

Caring for someone, on the other hand, can mean letting people stand on their own and holding them accountable for their actions. "Caring for" often means saying no: to raises when they haven't been earned, to promotions when they're not warranted, even for privileges when we know they're not healthy. Caring means being candid with others, even when it's uncomfortable doing so. To use the phrase widely quoted in debates about welfare: give people a hand up, not a handout.

We should care for other people because it's the right thing to do, but there are many other less-altruistic benefits as well. Doing good things for others increases the trust and affection others have for us and will likely make us feel happier and better about ourself. And by focusing attention on others, it helps dim the spotlight on our own ego.

Rely on Others

A final remedy for a case of Swollen Ego is to rely more on others. We all need people who ground us, who bring balance to our life, or who challenge us to be better versions of ourself. These can be family members, friends, employees, customers, suppliers, or professional colleagues. These people represent an incredible pool of ideas and inspiration if we are open and ready to listen. Deafness to the wisdom of others, unfortunately, is a key symptom of Swollen Ego.

We should be hearing a steady stream of feedback and input from the people around us. Our employees, and possibly our suppliers, should be bringing us ideas and inquiring about the things they see happening at our business when they question or don't understand them.

Warren Bennis, a pioneer in the field of leadership, writes "Authentic leaders ... don't have what people in the Middle East called 'tired ears.' Their egos are not so fragile that they are unable to bear the truth, however harsh—not because they are saints but because it is the surest way to succeed and survive." What business leader couldn't benefit from that kind of thinking?

When it comes to doing more listening to what they have to say, a spouse may be one of the most valuable people to start with. Our other half knows us better than anyone. And even if they aren't actively involved in the business, they probably have great insights into what goes on. This uniquely positions them to be the key person in our efforts to reduce a swollen ego. As someone who loves us, they can safely and confidently point out, "It is not all about you." A spouse can provide a crucial touchstone, helping us to stay grounded and to maintain perspective, and reminding us of all the people around us who have a huge stake in our business and success. That's certainly been true of my wife.

Hiring Good People

Of course, it doesn't make good business sense to listen to our employees if we've surrounded ourself with yes-men. As I described earlier, this is a common problem with Heroic Managers, but it's equally common with owners suffering from Swollen Ego. Since these owners are (in their minds) such towering examples of business brilliance, they don't need to rely on top-notch talent. Or they may worry about being outed as less towering than they put on and avoid hiring people who may show them up. Either way, their solution is to hire people who lack the smarts or nerve to contradict them.

A far better course of action comes from Malcolm Forbes who said, "Never hire someone who knows less than you do about what he's hired to do." We need to lower our shield, seek outside opinions and advice, and surround ourself with strong people who are willing to speak honestly to us.

Another way to approach this is to get involved in outside organizations, ideally at a board level. This could include civic, church, or industry-related organizations. It's easy to fancy ourself the smartest person in the room when we own the room and it's inside our business. But when we get involved with other talented people in outside organizations, we quickly gain perspective on our own capabilities and accomplishments. I know this from firsthand experience, having served on numerous industry and civic boards. These have provided me the chance to interact with people from different parts of the country, personal and professional backgrounds, and segments of industries. These have been tremendously valuable experiences, but it has also been humbling to interact with so many smart folks.

None of this is to suggest that we shouldn't have confidence in the decisions we make. We should and that's usually a big part of our job. We are in a unique position at the top of our organization. No one has a better overall perspective of the business, but we need to be cautious to not let that confidence grow into arrogance. We need to make sound choices and smart decisions based on all the information we can garner, not based on a misplaced and counterproductive need to feed our ego.

One final bit of advice regarding Swollen Egos taken from the Samurai and the martial art of jujutsu.[30] As stated earlier, almost every entrepreneur is afflicted to some extent by Swollen Ego, and that is something we can use to our advantage. Martial arts masters know that one of the secrets of success in battle is to turn the opponent's power against them. When they throw a punch, you don't try to stop or deflect it; you redirect the force, possibly leaving your opponent confused and flat on their back.

As I've described, a swollen ego can cause us to miss opportunities, overestimate our abilities, act impulsively, and just plain do dumb things. If we interact with any of our competitors, or if we keep tabs on them, we can probably recognize the signs of Swollen Ego from some of their actions. From a competitive standpoint, this can be a very valuable point to keep in mind if we are a younger or smaller company going up against a larger competitor.

Knowing that so many large, established companies fall victim to the perils of arrogance, ego, and entrenched thinking can be used to our advantage if we keep our minds and options open. Maybe something as simple as offering custom, out-of-the-box solutions to our customers' problems rather than saying, "That's not how we do it here" as the larger company might.

Checking Your Ego

Nothing compromises the long-term health and success of a business more than a swollen ego. An interesting thing about swelling is that it usually occurs when something has been injured. The swelling compensates for the injury but it doesn't actually heal the injury. It only masks the pain.

In much the same way, Swollen Ego is the mask that business owners wear to dull the pain of the previous five behaviors. It attempts to create the illusion that everything is going just fine when, in fact, it creates a situation similar to the band playing on as the *Titanic* sinks into the North Atlantic Ocean. The real dangers of Swollen Ego are that it not only causes owners to deny that problems exist in their business, but they also wall them off from the input, advice, and warnings of those around them. They have a ringside seat to the owner's self-destructive behavior but there's little they can do to prevent the unfortunate, eventual outcome.

Only when the owner can get that ego in check will they be able to see and acknowledge the areas of their business that need help and then seek assistance in correcting them. Until they do that, they are doomed to ignoring or being unaware of the dangers of the previous five behaviors. We don't need to possess the humility of Mother Teresa to succeed in business or in life, but someone with her humility and our business skills would probably be a force to reckon with. Most of us need to ramp up our self-awareness and recognize when our ego stops being a contributor and starts being an obstacle to our company's continued growth.

While it's possible to actually overcome or correct the other behaviors that make up the Entrepreneurial Conspiracy, that's usually not the case with Swollen Ego. In most cases, we can learn to manage it, but typically, we can't truly eliminate it. The exception are people who go through some highly emotional experiences, such as a bankruptcy or having to lay off employees who've been instrumental in building the business. These types of experiences, while traumatic, often provide a huge dose of humility that resets and resizes the person's ego.

Dwayne "The Rock" Johnson has every right to own a swollen ego, but his advice to others is, "Check your ego at the door. The ego can be the great success inhibitor. It can kill opportunities, and it can kill success."

CHAPTER 8

OVERCOMING THE CONSPIRACY

A s the saying goes, fish are the last to discover water. It's not much different with us and our personal behaviors. We're frequently the last to recognize the impact our behaviors have on the people around us and the effect they have on our life and on our business, both positive and negative.

The positive impact on our business is relatively easy to recognize, and it's usually not too difficult to draw a line connecting the business outcomes to the personal behaviors. But in our drive to hit KPIs or beat last year's numbers, we frequently overlook this connection.

Profits are consistently strong because we have talented people who are committed to earning them; we have talented and committed people because our company has a clearly articulated mission and direction that resonate with their personal and professional goals, and because our ego hasn't kept us from bringing strong players on board; our mission and direction are not only clearly articulated, but we're executing on them and holding our people and ourself accountable to achieve them; and we're executing on them because we're exhibiting the behavioral disciplines to establish our goals, act accountably, and maintain our focus through the myriad distractions every business leader encounters every day.

This is just one of countless examples of the positive outcomes when we successfully manage our Entrepreneurial Behaviors.

The negative outcomes of our behaviors on our business can be a little more difficult to connect. But just as with the positive outcomes, they do exist.

Naturally, there are an endless number of personal behavioral characteristics that contribute to either the success or the decline of our business. This book highlights just six. But they are six that I've seen repeated on a fairly regular basis across hundreds of small business owners running organizations ranging from startups to $100M.

Sometimes, it takes an outside observer to point out how our behaviors are perceived by the people around us and how those behaviors impact our business. The lucky ones among us have people in our lives who can point this out. Sometimes it's a loved one who cares about us. Sometimes it's a brave colleague who wants to see us succeed. Occasionally it's a business coach or consultant who's paid to give us candid, and sometimes bracing, feedback.

You no doubt noticed that among the remedies frequently mentioned in this book, one was to surround ourselves with "A" players. As I'm sure you've gathered, "A" players is a term I use to describe strong, competent people who are willing to speak the truth to authority. While this is helpful in every area of our life, it's particularly important in our business.

The larger our business grows, the more insulated we become from hearing the things we need to hear, especially from people within our own organization. Sometimes this happens because our people have concerns about their job security and won't tell us. They may feel we're unapproachable. Sometimes it's because they sense that we feel we're above hearing it. Regardless of the reason, this communication breakdown regarding the truth does nothing but lead to a company's ultimate decline.

If you recognized yourself in any of the pages of this book, then welcome to the party. You are not alone. As I frequently tell people, I write most of my material while looking in the mirror, and it seems I'm never at a loss for material to write about. That's why this book is primarily written in a first-person narrative.

For some, the temptation is to be overly critical of ourselves, to judge ourselves as inferior, or to compare ourselves to all the great business leaders we read so much about. Nothing is gained by making these comparisons, and that has not been my intention. Hopefully this temptation can be avoided.

The first step in managing or changing our behaviors is to recognize them. The next step is to accept ownership of the behaviors and take the necessary steps to correct them if they're harmful and continue them if they're helpful.

Barring a traumatic event, most of us can't address all the behaviors at one time and we won't make radical changes all at once. Lasting change takes time and sustained effort on our part. Quick fixes to deeply ingrained behaviors usually don't last. But what we can do is start.

We can take small steps toward improvement. Consistently put one foot in front of the other. Move the needle at least a little bit with every decision we make or with every interaction we have with others. Celebrate our small improvements. Learn from our setbacks. Keep moving forward.

If you don't see remarkable changes in your business overnight, don't get discouraged. Over time, you surely will.

In my own case, I was witnessing some of these behaviors in my clients before I recognized them in myself. It is usually much easier to notice other people's flaws than it is our own. I'd become frustrated because they always seemed to get distracted and wouldn't follow through on the things we had talked about (E-Drift; No Accountability). Or they wouldn't have the tough conversations with people that they had agreed to have (Hiding Out; No Accountability). Although I was initially frustrated by this, I soon noticed I was doing the same thing. And on closer examination, I realized that these behaviors were having exactly the same effect on my business that I was trying to correct in theirs. Doctor, heal thyself!

My only purpose in writing this book was to help the reader build a more successful business and a more rewarding life. By identifying personal behaviors within ourself that might be affecting the performance of our company, we can use this awareness to leverage the strengths of these behaviors and mitigate their weaknesses.

At no time have I suggested that you drop everything else you have going on and focus exclusively on becoming the model business leader. If you've owned a business for any length of time, you already know there are a multitude of responsibilities that demand our attention and that will influence the ultimate success or failure of our business.

Every day we have challenges and problems that require our immediate focus: conversations that can't wait until tomorrow, profits to be made, cash to be collected, employees to be hired and trained (or perhaps discharged), payrolls to meet, quality and service standards to exceed.

In addition to these daily demands on our time, there are forces acting on our business that are largely out of our control. Competitive pressures from other companies in our market, constantly shifting customer expectations and demands, economic pressures, governmental regulatory issues, and even the health and well-being of ourself and our loved ones.

All these responsibilities can be more effectively addressed if we have a better understanding of the six behaviors that will have an influence on how we address them. Some of the daily demands and outside forces may be out of our control, but we do have the ability to influence our own behaviors.

Here are five steps that can be taken to not only get started with changing the behaviors but to help you continue to make progress on them.

1. **Don't start until you're committed to the change.**
   Until you're ready to make real change in your behavior and in your business, I'd suggest you hold off on getting started.

   The process isn't going to be easy and there's a good chance it's going to be painful and frustrating. At times, you will probably become exhausted or discouraged and want to quit. But quitting would send the wrong message to the people around you.

   At other times, you'll think you're making great progress on one of the behaviors and someone will say something to the contrary. When this happens, it's easy to question whether it's all worth it. It is. And it might take all the energy you can muster to keep moving forward. Find that energy.

2. **Take baby steps.**
   Entrepreneurs aren't known for our lack of enthusiasm for new ideas or a lack of patience in making things happen. Avoid the temptation to jump in and try to address everything all at once and then expect to see miraculous results overnight. That's not how life works for most of us.

   At VMA we use the phrase "moving the needle" to describe making small, incremental progress toward a goal. It's a good approach for addressing these behaviors. Move your needle a bit every day.

3. **Keep moving forward.**
   I grew up in the American Midwest watching Big 10 football on Saturday afternoons. This was during a time before bright blue or red artificial surfaces were the norm; when games were played on real grass and most of that grass had been worn off the middle of the field by mid-season. It was a time when the expression used to describe making steady progress down the field was "three yards and a cloud of dust." It's no different with making steady progress toward changing a behavior.

Nobody's expecting to see miracles overnight. What our people want to see is a consistent effort, even if the improvement is minimal.

Entrepreneurs are famous for being strong starters but weak finishers. Too many initiatives fall apart because the owner gets bogged down in details, loses interest, or gets bored and moves onto the next new thing. Stay the course.

4. Expect to fall down along the way.

The Japanese proverb "Nana korobi ya oki" literally means "seven falls, eight getting up." In other words, it isn't whether you fall down seven times, it's whether you get back up eight.

The same is true with addressing these behaviors. In your quest to correct even one of them, expect to fall down. Maybe even seven times. What matters is whether you recommit the eighth time and try again.

None of us is perfect. We're all human. In spite of our best intentions, we're bound to backslide occasionally in our efforts to change our behaviors.

Managing change in any area of our life can be exhausting. Trying to change a behavior that we've spent a lifetime developing can drain our emotional batteries. Be sure to take the time to recharge them by acknowledging the successes you've had and the improvements that are being made in your company.

5. Get support.

This doesn't mean you need to form a support group and meet regularly to make sure you stay on track. Only in the most extreme situations would I suggest that. Instead, support can come in the form of letting the people around you know you're working to become a more effective leader by addressing these behaviors. Name them. Acquaint the people in your organization with their symptoms. Talk openly together about them, and ask others to let you know when you're exhibiting symptoms. This doesn't have to be punitive; make it fun and build a team to help you achieve your personal improvement goals.

The people in my organization know that I'm a charter member of the E-Drift club. I make no secret of it. Some dogs become exhausted chasing squirrels. This dog gets exhausted not chasing them. When my people see me doing this, it's not uncommon for them to ask, "Are we having an E-Drift moment here, boss?" Or, "Is this new idea somewhere in the Plan?"

I'm not sure I'll ever conquer this one, but I do work at getting better with it. And I rely on my people to help keep me on the rails. While this isn't always comfortable for me, I know it's a significant contributor to any success our organization has enjoyed.

I'm not convinced any of these behaviors are ever fixed. Instead, they are managed and modified during a lifelong journey. Some of them, like E-Drift and Swollen Ego, will require constant vigilance on our part to make sure they don't slowly reinsert themselves and once again start to cause damage.

Every human is a bundle of imperfections. Some of them are quaint and amusing and contribute to creating the unique personality that endears us to some people. Other imperfections are corrosive and destructive, driving people away, and hampering or destroying our potential to achieve personal happiness and business success.

Every one of us has the capacity for personal improvement and the ability to become a better version of ourself. While changing our behaviors may be difficult and painful at times, I can say with absolute certainty that you'll find it's worth the effort. And I hope you found some crumbs of inspiration in this book that will inspire, guide, and sustain you on the path to becoming that better version of yourself and a more-effective leader to your organization.

Good luck on your journey. Greater happiness, satisfaction, and business success lie ahead.

NOTES

[1] Those of you who are warm, caring, and generally nice may worry that traits like these won't serve you well as a leader, fearing there's truth in the axiom that "Nice guys finish last." Take heart, nice guys. An article in *Forbes* pointed out that success in business requires the support of your whole team and "Teams don't run too well with jerks. Unless you think you'll never need the assistance of anyone else, niceness is an investment that pays off in all areas of life." That's a nice thought.

[2] All client names are fictional or have been changed, sometimes hilariously.

[3] "Socializing" is a term I hear being used in large organizations to describe the process of sharing an idea or concept with others in the organization so they can start getting used to it. It's close to the older concept of "Run it up the flagpole and see if anyone salutes" but without the saluting. In this case, like the traditional notion of socializing, it's more about seeing how well the new idea fits in with the existing ideas that are part of your company's culture. Cocktails typically aren't part of this type of socializing, although serving them might increase adoption of the new idea.

[4] For those of you too young to know the origin of the reference Catch 22 (from the book and movie of the same name), it refers to a logic puzzle that's sometimes called a double bind. In the novel, set during World War II, people who were crazy were not obliged to fly missions. So some would go to the medical officer and ask to be released from missions because they were crazy. But anyone who applied to stop flying was showing a rational concern for their safety and, therefore, was sane. And that's a Catch 22. In the words of the character Doc Daneeka, "It's the best (catch) there is."

[5] For an amazing example of how sharp focus can actually cause us to miss important things, do an internet search for "selective attention test basketball

video." It demonstrates in a remarkable way how being unfocused can sometimes actually help us see things better.

6   Just as the wing of a plane performs the near magic of lifting the plane, the sail performs the remarkable feat of propelling a boat forward faster than the wind. The sailboat must be pointed toward the wind at an angle that varies with boat type, sail arrangement, and wind speed. In the 2013 America's Cup, a boat actually traveled at 50.8 mph in a wind of 18 mph, almost three times the speed of the wind.

7   The Schooner Lewis R. French is America's oldest windjammer, sailing since shortly after the death of Abraham Lincoln.

8   Some organizations and individuals don't feel the need to file their taxes, including a long list of celebrities. His $17 million penalty puts Willie Nelson at the top of the famous tax avoider heap. The same year his *Born for Trouble* album was released, the IRS seized almost everything Nelson owned with the exception of his favorite guitar, which his daughter nabbed before the agents arrived at his ranch. Nelson blamed his tax woes on his accounting firm, Price Waterhouse. It was later discovered that they had invested Nelson's funds rather than paying his taxes.

9   According to the Original Tooth Fairy Poll, conducted since 1998 by Delta Dental, the average gift left by the Tooth Fairy grew from $1.50 in 1998 to just over $4.00 in 2019. The poll collects average giving information and compares it to stock market activity to show how the value of a lost tooth correlates to the U.S. economy, providing the Tooth Fairy Index (SM). The two are closely related with one notable difference: the value of teeth dipped only slightly during the 2008 market crash, while major indices fell about 50%.

10   David Beckham consistently ranked among the highest earners in soccer and in 2013 he was listed as the highest-paid player in the world, earning over $50 million that year.

11   In a time when facts are few and far between in political speeches, politicians have this one right. Although only 22% of small businesses are employers, almost half of the country's private sector workforce works in a small business— about 120 million people. Since 1995, small businesses have created two out of

every three net new jobs. In the innovation front, small businesses produced 16 times more patents per employee than large firms.

[12]   This is one of the first best-selling self-help books ever published. It has sold more than 30 million copies and was #19 on *Time* magazine's list of The 100 Most Influential Books in 2011. Some of the key teachings include, "Become genuinely interested in other people," "Try honestly to see things from the other person's point of view," and "If you're wrong, admit it quickly and emphatically." There's little doubt that a world governed by the rules laid down in Carnegie's book would be a better world. A recent resurgence in Dale Carnegie training points to the timelessness of his simple advice.

[13]   Formerly known as "tellers" from an Old English word that meant "to count." As in a number of occupations, the titles have grown bigger and fancier as the compensation and job security declined. Secretaries are administrative assistants, store guards are loss-prevention officers, sales people are customer service associates, and receptionists are managers of first impressions.

[14]   Lee made cameo appearances in many of the Marvel films. Thanks to the huge box office from those films, Lee has the distinction of holding the number one spot in terms of total revenue generated by all the films an actor has appeared in over their lifetime.

[15]   In the mid-1950s, phone booth stuffing was a popular fad. In 1959, 25 students in South Africa set a world record when each squeezed most of his body into a standard phone booth.

[16]   The word *robot* was first used to denote a fictional humanoid in a 1920 play by a Czech writer. The word comes from the Czech "robota" which means forced work or labor. The most common domestic use of robots is to sweep the floor, which was an exciting development in the early 2000s for nerdy homeowners with deep pockets. These automated vacuums now have advanced features such as laser navigation and Wi-Fi connectivity, making it much less likely that you will find one stuck in a corner or wedged under the couch. Despite their advances, they are still far away from the far-more-functional humanoid domestic helpers depicted in movies.

[17]   The abstract of the research document describing this phenomenon states it in some highly clinical terms. The study "employed normalization models

to predict context dependence of facial attractiveness preferences. Divisive normalization—where representation of stimulus intensity is normalized (divided) by concurrent stimulus intensities—predicts that choice preferences between options increase with the range of option values. The more unattractive the distractors, the more one of the targets was preferred, suggesting that divisive normalization (a potential canonical computation in the brain) influences social evaluations." The bottom line: find a homely wingman.

[18] A sales consultant receives a car when they and their team reach $100,000 in sales within a year. The car, however, isn't actually an outright gift. They have it on a two-year co-op lease paid for by Mary Kay. When the two years is up, the consultant can opt to sell the car back to the dealership or purchase it.

[19] Blimps are notoriously difficult to learn to fly, in part because they are so slow to respond to any change in controls. Pilots push the controls forward and wait … and wait … for the blimp to go down. Add to that the very strong effect wind has on blimps due to their huge size and low mass and smooth flights become even more difficult. With less than 40 blimp pilots in the world, it's one of the rarest jobs on the planet.

[20] www.forbes.com/sites/lisaquast/2017/02/06/want-to-be-more-productive-stop-multi-tasking/#5222077055a6

[21] Chutzpah comes from a Yiddish word that originally meant insolence or audacity and had a strongly negative connotation. Today, when we use it in English to describe people in business, it has taken on the meaning of nerve or courage with a positive connotation. There's no doubt that betting the future for you and your family on a business that you launch required chutzpah.

[22] The honcho is a leader or manager; the person in charge. It is a Japanese word, often mistakenly thought to be of Spanish origin, originally referring to a small-time yakuza (Japanese mafia) gangster in charge of just a few underlings. The underworld connotation has been lost as the word has been adopted into English. The term came home with U.S. servicemen who were stationed in Japan during the occupation following the Second World War.

[23] These are the starting and ending points for the Cannonball Run, conducted several times during the 1970s and honored in the movie by the same name. There were no rules regarding routes, vehicles, drivers, or speeds. Participants

agreed that the vehicle entered would be driven the entire distance. The record is 32 hours and 51 minutes (an average of about 87 mph) set in 1979 in the final run by a Jaguar XJS.

[24] I would actually have guessed that the worst disease afflicting business executives is workaholism.

[25] www.scientificamerican.com/article/how-wealth-reduces-compassion

[26] hbr.org/2015/04/how-emotional-intelligence-became-a-key-leadership-skill

[27] time.com/3593413/emotional-intelligence-salary

[28] The "Ides of March" refers to a day, or a period, on the Roman calendar. Back then, they didn't number days of the month from the first through the last day. Instead, months were divided into day markers that fell at the start of the month (calends), the fifth or seventh day (nones), and the middle of the month (ides). Then you counted backward from those markers. The calends occurred on the day of the new moon. This cumbersome approach was later replaced by the Julian Calendar (which is still followed by some religions) and later the Gregorian Calendar, which is what we use today.

[29] "The catbird seat" is an American English phrase meant to describe an enviable position, including having the upper hand or great advantage. It refers to the fact that catbirds seek out the highest perches in trees to sing and display. The Oxford English Dictionary says the first recorded usage of the phrase was in a 1942 humorous short story by James Thurber titled "The Catbird Seat." It was then popularized by legendary sports announcer Red Barber. If you prefer not to sit in the catbird seat, the phrase "sitting pretty" has a similar meaning.

[30] The word Jujutsu, aka Jiu-Jitsu and Ju-Jitsu, can be broken down into two parts. "Ju" means to give way or yield and "Jutsu" means science or art. Jujutsu is based on using your opponent's force against themself rather than confronting it with your own force. It includes throwing, immobilizing, and choking techniques. Karate is a largely different style, based on striking the opponent, but this technique became less effective on the battlefield as combatants increased the use of armor.

REFERENCE SOURCES

Chapter 1—Behave Yourself

Groundhog Day—Movie

What Got You Here Won't Get You There—Marshall Goldsmith

The Founder's Mentality—Chris Zook/James Allen

Chapter 2—Blurred Vision

Catch 22—Joseph Heller

Good to Great—Jim Collins

The Fifth Discipline—Peter Senge

Start With Why—Simon Sinek

Ego is the Enemy—Ryan Holiday

Flight of the Buffalo—James A Belasco and Ralph C Stayer

Falling Upward—Richard Rohr

How the Mighty Fall—Jim Collins

The Founder's Mentality—Chris Zook/James Allen

The Fifth Discipline—Peter Senge

Groundhog Day—Movie, chapter 1

What Got You Here Won't Get You There—Marshall Goldsmith

Chapter 3—No Accountability

The Pursuit of Prime—Dr. Ichak Adizes

Winnie the Pooh—A.A. Milne

Good to Great—Jim Collins

The E Myth—Michael Gerber

How to Win Friends and Influence People—Dale Carnegie

The Fifth Discipline—Peter Senge

Start With Why—Simon Sinek

Extreme Ownership: How U.S. Navy SEALs Lead and Win—Jocko Willink and Leif Babin

Chapter 4—Heroic Managing

The Peter Principal—Laurence J Peter/Raymond Hull
Beyond Survival—Leon Danco
The Pursuit of Prime—Dr. Ichak Adizes
Flight of the Buffalo—James A Belasco and Ralph C Stayer

Chapter 5—E-Drift

The E-Myth—Michael E Gerber
Article in Contractor Cents, "The Mercedes-Benz Syndrome"—Ruth King
How the Mighty Fall—Jim Collins

Chapter 6—Hiding Out

Crucial Conversations: Tools for Talking When Stakes are High—Kerry Patterson, Joseph
Grenny, Ron McMillan, Al Switzler
Radical Candor: Be a Kick Ass Boss Without Losing Your Humanity—Kim Scott

Chapter 7—Swollen Ego

How the Mighty Fall—Jim Collins
The Founders Mentality—Chris Zook/James Allen
Mind Set!—John Naisbitt
Rutgers University—Study
Article in Scientific American, "How Wealth Reduces Compassion"—Daisy Grewal
Article in Harvard Business Review—Andrea Evans
Falling Upward—Richard Rohr
Ego is the Enemy—Ryan Holiday
Freakanomics—Steven D. Levitt/Stephen J. Dubner
Primal Leadership—Daniel Goleman, Richard Boyatzis, Annie McKee
Extreme Ownership: How U.S. Navy SEALs Lead and Win—Jocko Willink and Leif Babin
The Humility Imperative: Why the Humble Leader Wins In an Age of Ego—Andrew Kerr
What Got You Here Won't Get You There—Marshall Goldsmith
Leaders Eat Last—Simon Sinek
Return on Character: The Real Reason Leaders and Their Companies Win—Fred Kiel
How to Win Friends and Influence People—Dale Carnegie
Working Without a Net: How to Survive and Thrive in Today's High Risk Business World—
Morris R Shechtman

ABOUT THE AUTHOR

Chuck Violand is the founder and principal of Violand Management Associates, LLC (VMA), a consulting company working internationally throughout the United States, Canada, and Australia, whose focus is on small businesses.

Chuck started VMA in 1987 to help small businesses achieve sustained profitable growth and to help their owners and management teams achieve long-term professional and personal success.

As an author and popular keynote speaker, Chuck is a respected authority on the unique challenges faced by entrepreneurial small businesses, having spent over thirty years as a business consultant and an executive coach. He is a regular contributor to trade publications and newsletters in addition to authoring his popular, weekly leadership series *Monday Morning Notes*.

In his more than 50 years of business, Chuck's varied experiences include having owned nightclubs, a food processing company, and contracting companies. Today, he continues to play an active role at VMA.

Chuck and his wife, Karen, are the parents of four adult children and reside in Northeast Ohio.